Samuel H. Walker's Account
of the Mier Expedition

The publication of this book was made possible through a grant from the Pate Foundation, Fort Worth, Texas: A. M. Pate, Jr., President; Sebert L. Pate, Vice-President.

Samuel H. Walker's Account of the Mier Expedition

Edited with an Introduction by
Marilyn McAdams Sibley

THE TEXAS STATE HISTORICAL ASSOCIATION

CONTENTS

ILLUSTRATIONS

Samuel H. Walker's Account
of the Mier Expedition

INTRODUCTION

THE TEXAS RANGERS called him Unlucky Walker,[1] and in some respects Samuel Hamilton Walker deserved the name. He joined the disastrous Mier Expedition and ended up a prisoner in Mexico; he was wounded regularly in Ranger battles with the Indians; and finally he died leading an assault during the Mexican War.

Even so, Walker was more fortunate than many men. When the Mier prisoners drew beans to determine who lived or died, he drew a white bean, meaning life; he lived to fight again after receiving wounds that would have killed or disabled most mortals; and he died at the peak of his career and at the point of victory. In addition, Walker popularized the sensational new weapon of his era, giving his name to a variation of the Colt revolver.

Walker's mixed luck carried over into his literary production. He kept a journal of the Mier Expedition, but despite his later re-

Thomas Jefferson Green used Walker's diary as the nucleus of his *Journal of the Texian Expedition Against Mier* (1845).

nown and the enduring interest in the black bean episode, the existence of his journal has remained unknown.[2]

In one respect, however, Walker's account may be the best known of all accounts of the expedition, for it is incorporated into the standard work on the subject—Thomas Jefferson Green's *Journal of the Texian Expedition against Mier*. Walker handed the journal to Green after both men had returned to Texas. Green used it as the nucleus to which he added his own recollections, correspondence, and a great deal of editorial comment, but he published the book in 1845 without a line of credit to Walker and only scant mention of him. That Green did so tells something of his own character. A pompous, self-important snob, he customarily gave little consideration to those who could not further his own ends, and he served as an officer on the Mier Expedition while Walker served as an obscure private.

Nor was there any evidence then that Walker would become the proverbial legend in his own time. His fame came in the few years of life left to him after he gave his journal to Green. The Rangers appreciated Walker's bravery but did not single him out for honor until after the Mexican War began, and even at the height of his fame, friendly observers found little in his personal appearance to denote the hero. "He was about medium size, with light hair and a mild expression of countenance," said one acquaintance, while another observed that "his intellect was mediocre and not much cultivated," and yet another called him "an ordinary man in ordinary service; retiring, silent, mild, apathetic, and rather melancholy."[3]

But all agreed that in action Walker was a born warrior. One comrade called him the "thunderboldt of the Texas Rangers," and another the "bravest of the brave," and when he died his men, all hardened fighters, "wept like children, and their stout hearts were melted."[4] A fellow soldier wrote his epitaph: "War was his element, the bivouac his delight, and the battlefield his playground, his perfection and inspiration."[5]

Despite Walker's fame, the facts about his early life are sketchy. No book-length biography has been written of him, and much that has been printed about him is erroneous or distorted. The son of Nathan and Elizabeth Walker, he was born in Prince George County, Maryland, about 1815. His parents having a large family

6

Samuel H. Walker, from a daguerreotype by J. McGuire, New Orleans.

and being of modest means, he became a carpenters' apprentice at an early age. That trade held little attraction for him, and, when Indian troubles developed in Florida in the early 1830's, he marched off to war with a group of Washington volunteers. After his enlistment expired, he served for a time as a scout along the Appalachicola River and later as a superintendent of a railroad.[6] Then the promise of adventure lured him to Texas.

Walker arrived at Galveston in January, 1842,[7] and from then until his death his career is well documented. His own journal, which follows, tells of his first eventful year in Texas and of his subsequent trials in Mexico; his later career emerges in the annals of the Texas Rangers, his correspondence with Samuel Colt, and the records of the Mexican War.

As Walker relates in his journal, he arrived in Texas in time to participate in the major episodes of an eventful season. Mexico never recognized the Republic of Texas, and from its founding in 1836 the Republic led a precarious existence, under constant threat of Mexican invasion and Indian raids. In 1841 the Texans compounded their problems by sending the Santa Fe Expedition to New Mexico. In retaliation, Mexico launched several actions against Texas in 1842, sending General Rafael Vásquez to raid San Antonio in April and General Adrian Woll against the same city in September.[8]

Walker joined those who rallied to the defense, and he distinguished himself in the actions around San Antonio after the Woll raid. He and his fellows remained eager for aggressive action against Mexico, but President Sam Houston, knowing the weaknesses of the Republic, seemed reluctant to authorize it. Finally in October, Houston yielded to public pressure and appointed Alexander Somervell to lead an expedition toward the Rio Grande.

Walker joined that expedition and participated in the actions around Laredo and Guerrero. Somervell then ordered the men to return home, whereupon some three hundred of them, including

Walker, protested and, organizing a rump expedition under William S. Fisher, attacked the Mexican town of Mier. They were defeated, captured, and marched toward Mexico City. At the village of Salado, the main body of them escaped, but after much suffering they were recaptured. As punishment Santa Anna ordered that one in ten be executed, and there followed the drawing of beans from a jar to determine who should die.

Green was not with the main body of men during these most dramatic of their trials, and it is for this portion of his book that he is most indebted to Walker's journal. Green's book, in turn, jogged the memories of other survivors and influenced their writings,[9] so that Walker's journal exerted more influence than most little-known manuscripts.

At least some of the problems of the Mier men stemmed from their manner of entering Mexico. "It is true the men went without orders," President Sam Houston wrote the British minister, "and so far as that was concerned, the Government of Texas was not responsible; and the men thereby placed themselves out of the protection of the rules of war."[10] Houston went on to ask the minister's help in freeing the men, but many Texans did not read beyond his introductory statements. They charged that Houston caused the decimation at Salado by disclaiming responsibility for the men, and the matter became a volatile political issue on the eve of the last presidential election in the Republic.

Possibly because of the political repercussions, both the Somervell and Mier men generally received a bad press. Some of them were "brokendown politicians from the 'Old States,' that somehow had got on the wrong side of the fence and been left out in the cold," recalled "Big-Foot" Wallace, himself a participant. Others he described as "renegades and refugees from justice that had 'left their country for their country's good,' and adventurers of all sorts, ready for anything or any enterprise that afforded a reasonable prospect of excitement and plunder."[11]

But some of the men could claim distinction. Sam Walker and Big-Foot Wallace became legendary as Texas Rangers, as did Jack Hays and Ben McCulloch; McCulloch and George B. Crittenden became Confederate generals; Memucan Hunt had served as secretary of the Texas navy and represented the Republic in the United States; Peter Hansborough Bell, also a Texas Ranger, would become governor of Texas; and Thomas Jefferson Green, controversial and tempestuous, could eventually boast of serving in the legislative bodies of four states.

But no reputations were made in the Somervell Expedition or its offshoot, the Mier Expedition. The first ended in futility, and the latter in tragedy. Both resulted in recrimination and bitterness as the men charged their leaders with timidity, their government with perfidy, and each other with plundering and disloyalty. The affair produced martyrs but little in the way of heroes.

This is the story Walker tells in his journal. He begins with a narrative account of the early campaigns of 1842, possibly written at least some time after the event. But after his capture at Mier he began a day-by-day record for obvious reasons: escape was uppermost in his mind, and by a careful notation of distances and landmarks he could use the journal as a guide for returning home. Later, as the prisoners moved further into Mexico and their misfortunes multiplied, he recorded the fates of his companions so that, if he did return, he could give dates and places to their next of kin, and so, if the opportunity arose, he could take vengeance.

After the decimation at Salado, Walker was imprisoned at Tacubaya, a suburb of Mexico City, where he and his fellows built a road leading to Santa Anna's palace. While there Walker suffered a severe beating by a guard, and learned through Waddy Thompson, the United States minister to Mexico, of Sam Houston's disclaiming responsibility for the Mier men. Walker ends his journal with an account of his successful escape.[12]

Contrary to some accounts, the journal indicates that Walker was never imprisoned at Perote Castle. Nor does the journal give any basis for a story widely circulated during the Mexican War that at one point in his captivity Walker was forced to erect a flag-pole. According to the story, he put a dime under the pole, promising that he would return for it, and, although his captors laughed at the time, he retrieved the dime when he returned with the invading army.[13]

That story is probably apocryphal, but the journal explains in good measure why during the Mexican War Walker returned with such fury to the scenes of his suffering. He was a simple man with an Old Testament sense of vengeance, and he became the terror of the citizenry. "The renowned Captain Samuel H. Walker takes no prisoners," wrote an American soldier on one occasion, and on another, "Should Captain Walker come across guerrillas God help them for he seldom brings in prisoners."[14]

Before Walker wreaked his vengeance on Mexico, he achieved vengeance of a different kind against another whom he held responsible for his suffering. He escaped from prison full of bitterness toward Sam Houston. Shortly after his return to Texas, he confronted Houston, charging that the president was responsible for the decimation at Salado because of his statements to the British diplomat. Houston denied making such statements, asked Walker the source of the charges, and upon being informed that Waddy Thompson had made them, asked that the charges be put in writing.

Walker complied with the request, writing a letter that came close to calling Houston a liar:

As your Excellency denied the truth of these statements and accused General Thompson of falsehood in our conversation the other day, the issue of truth or falsehood is between you. . . . If they are untrue General Thompson would justly sink in the estimation of every honest man and prove to the world that high and honourable office will not prevent men from lieing . . .

As one of the prisoners who suffered from the report, whether true or false, I wish not only to be satisfied myself but to satisfy all who doubt. Will your Excellency have the kindness to introduce me to Captain Elliott that I may hear his denial in your presence of any authority from you to make statements said to be contained in his dispatch to Mr. Packenham?[15]

Houston refused to answer the letter,[16] but about this time, he met Walker on a staircase in Galveston and extended his hand. Walker ignored the gesture and continued on his way, while Houston, with his characteristic aplomb, stopped for a moment and then called over his shoulder, "I am very sorry you are indisposed, Mr. Walker."[17]

Thomas Jefferson Green, who escaped from Mexico shortly before Walker, heard of Walker's confrontation with Houston and asked for a record of it.[18] Green and Walker were not well acquainted. Green, along with most of the officers, had been imprisoned at Perote rather than Tacubaya, and he figures as inconspicuously in Walker's journal as Walker does in his book. But the two agreed in regard to Sam Houston. Walker deposited a record of his dealings with Houston and the journal with Green and then departed for the frontier.

In Green's hands, the journal grew into a book that voiced the bitterness of the Mier survivors toward Houston. Indeed, the book is almost as much a tirade against Houston as it is a record of the expedition. Houston was stung by it and felt called upon to defend himself publicly.[19] Green refused to let the matter drop, and the two carried on a vicious word battle for a decade.[20]

Thus, Walker's journal served his purpose at the time, even though he has been neglected by history because of Green's failure to give proper credit. From a practical viewpoint, the fact that Walker's name was not prominently associated with the book is probably fortunate, for within two years after it appeared he needed Houston's help. Houston was then senator from Texas and

Walker a war hero; Walker asked for and received the senator's help in persuading the United States War Department to purchase Colt revolvers.[21]

By the time Green's book appeared, Walker was on the Texas frontier earning his reputation for fearlessness and experimenting with the gun that would bring him lasting fame. Early in 1844 the Texas Congress authorized John Coffee Hays to organize a company of Rangers to protect the west from Indians. Hays obtained a few Colt revolvers which the Republic ordered for the Texas navy before Sam Colt, the developer of the weapons, fell into bankruptcy.[22] Walker joined Hays' company and, with the other Rangers, practiced with the revolver. Then the Rangers, made bold by their new weapons, took on several times their number of Indians in a battle on the Pedernales River.

Walter Prescott Webb has pointed to the battle as a landmark in frontier warfare because of the use of the revolvers,[23] and Walker later described it to Sam Colt:

In the Summer of 1844 Col. J. C. Hays with fifteen men fought about eighty Comanche Indians, boldly attacking them upon their own ground, killing and wounding about half their number. Up to this time these daring Indians had always supposed themselves superior to us, man to man, on horse—at that time they were threatening a descent upon our Frontier Settlements—the result of this engagement was such as to intimidate them and enable us to treat with them. Several other Skirmishes have been equally satisfactory, and I can safely say that you deserve a large share of the credit for success. Without your pistols we would not have had the confidence to have undertaken such daring adventures.[24]

Others have described this battle more vividly,[25] but Walker's description was enough for Sam Colt. He immortalized it with an engraving, signed by W. L. Ormsby, which later appeared on some early revolvers.[26]

Walker was seriously wounded in the battle, but after a long

Courtesy Connecticut State Library Collection
Gus Johnson, Photographer

This engraving on the cylinder of a Colt pistol depicts the battle on the Pedernales in which fifteen Texas Rangers armed with revolvers defeated about eighty Indians. Jack Hays and Sam Walker are pictured on horseback right.

convalescence he recovered in time to receive additional wounds in other battles and earn his sobriquet Unlucky Walker.[27] His adventures on the frontier, however, served only as preparation for the next—and last—chapter of his life.

In 1845 the United States annexed Texas, which Mexico still claimed, and sent Zachary Taylor's army to Corpus Christi to meet any objections. The promise of action drew Walker to Corpus Christi, where he organized a company of Texas Mounted Rangers to act as scouts for Taylor's army. As hostilities began, Walker rendered invaluable services which were highly publicized by the national press.[28] He caught the public fancy and, along with Zachary Taylor, became one of the early heroes of the Mexican War.

After the declaration of war, Jack Hays organized a regiment of Texas Rangers, of which Walker was lieutenant colonel. The Rangers joined Taylor's army for the battle of Monterrey, distinguishing themselves in action. At a crucial point in the battle they fought from house to house with Hays taking the right side of the street and Walker the left.[29] Walter P. Lane, who served with Walker, later recalled that by nightfall they had fought their way to within fifty yards of the main plaza. "Col. Walker and myself had the honor of sleeping in Gen. Ampudia's bed, their commander-in-chief, whom we had just routed out of his quarters," Lane wrote.[30]

Shortly after the battle of Monterrey, Walker accepted a commission as captain in the United States army. He returned to Maryland to recruit his men and enjoy the attention that his new status brought him.

At this point in the fall of 1846, he first came in contact with Sam Colt.[31] Despite financial problems, Colt still had faith in his revolver and eagerly sought endorsement of it by prominent figures. He wrote Walker a letter inviting praise and displaying his own peculiarities of spelling:

I have hard so much of Col Hayse & your exployets with the Arms of my invention that I have long desired to know you personally & get from you a true narrative of the vareous instances where my arms have proved of more the ordinary utility . . . I hope your will favour by with a minute detail of all occasions where you have used & seen my arms of ordinary construction . . . I have no doubt that with the hints which I may get from you & others having experience in there use in the field that they can be made the most complete thing in the world.[32]

Walker replied with an account of the battle on the Pedernales, concluding his letter with, "The people throughout Texas are anxious to procure your pistols & I doubt not you would find sale for a large number at this time."[33] He was not, however, completely satisfied with the revolvers. Along with his praise, he included the sentence, "With improvements I think they can be rendered the most perfect weapon in the World for light mounted troops."[34]

Colt arranged for a meeting and asked Walker to be more spe-

Courtesy Wadsworth Atheneum, Hartford, Colt Collection
Samuel Colt sent this pistol to Samuel H. Walker in Mexico. After Walker's
death, Bedney F. McDonald returned it to Colt.

cific about the improvements. Again Walker complied. A man
fighting on horseback needed a weapon with a trigger guard and
an improved loading device so he would not lose a part of his gun
when reloading. And the gun should be heavier so he could use it
as a club after he exhausted his ammunition.

The meeting was momentous for both men. Colt designed the
new weapon and named it the Walker Colt revolver, thus giving
Walker his claim to enduring fame. Walker returned the favor by
persuading the War Department to order a thousand of the weapons, thus giving Colt the boost he needed to break with his past
failures and become a successful arms manufacturer.

Colt did not even have a factory when he contracted for the
guns. He negotiated with Eli Whitney for their manufacture, and
Walker could not wait for them.[35] He received orders to return to

Death of Samuel H. Walker at Battle of Huamantla, as depicted in J. J. Oswandel, *Notes of the Mexican War* (1885).

Mexico, which he did, sending Colt letter after letter imploring him to hasten production of the weapons.[36]

In early October, 1847, Walker received the first two of the new revolvers and expressed delight with them. "I have just received a pair of Colts Pistols which he sent to me as a present," he wrote his brother on October 5. "There is not an officer who has seen them but what speaks in the highest terms of them and all of the

Cavalry officers are determined to get them if possible. Col. Harney says they are the best arm in the world."[37]

Four days later, on October 9, Walker died in battle at Huamantla at the age of thirty-two. His death brought an outpouring of grief nationwide. His men went on a rampage, avenging his death in the same manner that he had avenged the death of his Mier comrades. "His men resolved that from this out that they would take no prisoners, and death to all Mexicans found with firearms in their hands," wrote an American soldier. "They charged after the retreating army of Gen. Santa Anna, overtook them, and killed several hundred of the enemy. The carnage, they say, was awful—cutting the enemy down right and left, just like a mower cutting grass or grain."[38] Walker's exploits were further enhanced by the national press, and his legend grew with the appearance of such works as *The Brave Ranger*, which Samuel Bangs published in Matamoros and which was recognized as "puff" during its own time.[39]

Nine years later on April 21, 1856, following a formal mourning period, Walker's remains were reburied in the Odd Fellows' Cemetery at San Antonio as a part of the San Jacinto Day celebration. Appropriately, he was buried beside his fellow Ranger, Robert Addison Gillespie, who fell at Monterrey, and the eulogy was delivered by James Charles Wilson, who escaped with him from prison in Tacubaya.[40]

Memorabilia of Walker is scattered. His right-hand revolver, Walker Colt No. 1020, was returned to Sam Colt. It became the prize of Colt's collection, and eventually his widow deposited it in the Wadsworth Atheneum, Hartford, Connecticut. Two of his other personal weapons, Walker Colt revolvers Nos. 1009 and 1010, were sent to his family. One still remains in family hands; the other was acquired in the 1940's by a collector in California. His sword was given to Philip F. Bowman, who suffered with him in the Mier Expedition and returned as a major in the First Penn-

This monument in the Odd Fellows' Cemetery at San Antonio bears the inscription "To the Memory of Capt. R. A. Gillespie & Capt. S. H. Walker by their Comrades in Arms." The smaller marker to the left rear is Walker's gravestone.

A fellow soldier preserved Walker's sword. "The scabbard is deeply indented, the edge of the blade is hacked, and on the inner side of the well-worn belt appears, amidst blood stains, the name, written by his own hand, of Samuel H. Walker," wrote Edmund L. Dana.

sylvania Regiment to fight with him during the Mexican War. Bowman deposited the sword in the museum of the Wyoming Historical Society at Wilkes-Barre, Pennsylvania.[41]

Walker's journal of the Mier Expedition remained with Thomas Jefferson Green's papers and eventually was deposited with them in the archives of the University of North Carolina, where it rested unnoticed until the present.

As the key portions were appropriated by Green, the journal tells little new about the escape at Salado, its ultimate failure, and the drawing of the black beans. It subsequently follows the men imprisoned at Tacubaya, however, while Green follows those at Perote. Thus, it depicts the experiences of another group of captives. In addition, it tells a great deal about the simple fighting man who wrote it and whose legend is better known than he.

Walker's original spelling is retained in the transcription, but punctuation is added when necessary for clarity. His original title is also retained.

SAM'L H. WALKER:
MEMORANDUM BOOK
YEAR OF OUR LORD 1842

O N THE 6TH OF MARCH 1842 Gen. Bascus [Rafael Vásquez] entered and took possession of Bexar with about 700 troops without resistance, having induced the Texians whose force was small to believe that his force was the advance guard of a large invading army.

The Texians to about 3,000 in number soon rallied to the frontier to meet the supposed invading forces but we were much disappointed as it proved only to be a marauding party authorised by the government of Mexico. Their stay was short and their retreat hasty. Their inroad however was marked with pillage and plunder, taking with them about $30,000 worth of goods.[42]

The most of the Texians were anxious to pursue the enemy across the Rio Grande, but the discontent was occasioned by Sam Houston endeavouring to place Gen. Somerville [Alexander Somervell] in command because he was the militia Genl of the western district. The volunteers would not then acknowledge Houston's right to appoint a commander of Somerville's ability to command an invading force. The expedition was given up and the Texians returned to their homes with loud curses against Sam Houston.

But scarcely had they reached their homes when Sam Houston's celebrated reply to Santa Anna made its appearance.[43] It was written in the language of a statesman and a patriot and of course pleased the people and made them satisfied to wait until an expedition could be got up under the sanction & patronage of the executive. The call was made to the friends of Texas in the U.S. and many of them were in short time landed in Texas ready, armed, & equipped for active service, but in return for their patriotism they received very cool and disrespectful treatment from Sam Houston and eventually returned without compensation or thanks for their service, fully convinced that the immortal hero of San Jacinto was more smoke than fire because he had complained in the first place that Congress had not given him the authority to use the public lands which were the principle resources of the Government.

Meanwhile he called Congress together and after they had given him the authority which they supposed he wanted he vetoed the bill on the grounds that it was unconstitutional and some future aspirant might use such authority to the destruction of the liberties of his country. Congress then passed a bill giving him authority to authorise volunteer expeditions into the enemies' country and commission such officers as should be duly elected by the organized companies at the sulpher springs on the Cibola, the place of rendezvous. He accordingly published his proclamation, but it had not become generally known before another report was in circulation that the executive of the U.S. had requested a cessation of hostilities and would endeavour to use her influence to make an amicable settlement of the differences between the two countries. It was reported that Sam Houston intended to recall the navy, and neither would he allow the expedition which he had authorised to cross the Rio Grande, but he denied having made any such insinuation and expressed a wish that the people would turn out, cross the Rio Grande and chastise the enemy for their depredations on Bexar. The people however had lost all confidence of anything being done under Houston's management and therefore would not turn out in sufficient numbers to make a campaign.

On the 7th of July Gen. Canalles [Antonio Canales] with one piece of artillery, 500 cavalry, & 200 infantry attacked about 180 volunteers principally from the U.S. on the banks of the Nueces River at a place called Lipantitlan. They made several charges but were easily repulsed by the volunteers, who had not a man hurt. Much credit is due to Capt. [Ewen] Cameron in this affair. The enemy left 4 men on the field besides some 8 or 10 wounded which they took off. It so happened, however, that Gen. Canalles claimed a decisive victory from the following circumstances. The volunteers had heard so many reports of the Mexicans that they at last got so they would not believe any such reports. Houston had neglected to feed them and for several days previous they had been without food. The consequence was they had become reckless & careless and when they were informed on the evening of the 6th of July of the approach of the enemy, it was with some difficulty that Gen. [James] Davis, the commander, could prevail on the Texians to take the precaution to move to a more advantagous position, leaving their camp equipage and everything in the old camp, intending to return early in the morning. The night was passed a few hundred yards off and at daylight on the 7th as the volunteers were returning to their former camp, they found it surrounded by the enemy who opened a fire on them with their field piece. The Texians fell back to their chosen position where they had spent the night, leaving their banners and camp equipage in the hands of the enemy which enabled Canalles to palm his deception on the people of the country that he had gained a decisive victory over 500 Texians.[44]

Thus ended the campaign of Canalles whose victory was celebrated throughout all Mexico.

On the 11th of Sept. Gen. [Adrian] Woll entered and took possession of Bexar after a slight resistance. Court was sitting and the Texans in Bexar had some warning of his approach but were disposed to believe that it was another robbing party like that commanded by Bascus. They accordingly sent commissioners to meet him and inquire of him whether he came as a robber or as a warrior under the authority of his Government. If the former, the Mexican citizens of Bexar expressed a determination to defend the place in concert with the Texians about sixty in number. If the latter, they desired the commissioners to say that he would meet with non resistance. But instead of his letting the commissioners return, he detained them and entered the town at daybreak in the morning of the 11th with 700 cavalry, 600 infantry & 2 pieces of artillery. He was a little surprised when a fire from about 53 Texians killed 6 & wounded 23 of his men, killing the General's horse from under him and also several others of his staff, and after withdrawing from the square and cannonading a short time, he sent in a flag and offered to treat the Texians as prisoners of war if they would surrender. Amongst them was several of the Santa Fe prisoners who were named and were also assured they should be treated as prisoners of war. These prisoners were in a short time sent off to Mexico. The news reached the Colorado on the 14th and the Texians again supposed this to be the vanguard of a large invading army.[45]

On the 18th of Sept., Col. [Mathew] Caldwell took a position on the Salado within 5 miles of Bexar with 202 men.[46] He sent Capt. [John Coffee] Hays with fifty horsemen to the suburbs of the town to draw out the enemy, which succeeded. Hays rejoined

Caldwell on the Salado, pursued by the whole force joined by about 200 Bexar Mexicans. The fight continued until about four o'clock with very trifling loss to the Texians and considerable loss to the enemy.[47] At this time Capt. [Nicholas] Dawson imprudently advanced in the open prairie with 53 men, and, making a stand rather than retreat, the cannon was brought to bear on him: 33 of his men killed, 18 wounded and taken prisoners, 2 only making their escape. They made considerable slaughter, however, amongst the enemy. Dawson, after finding he had got in a situation from which he could not extricate himself, hoisted a white flag and asked for quarter but was refused and many of them died fighting hand to hand with the enemy. The reason given by the Mexicans for refusing quarter to these brave men was that Caldwell had refused to receive a white flag from them, which was a poor reason as they never ceased firing when they sent their flag to Caldwell and besides it was to demand a surrender.

On the same evening Capt. Billingsly's [Jesse Billingsley's] company arrived just in time to witness the closing scene of the action with 75 men but, deeming it imprudent to advance on the enemy, fell back a few miles to await reinforcements.[48]

I had in the meanwhile reconnoitered the enemy and also gained some idea of Caldwell's position, in which I learned to appreciate the value of good stock. My horse was well tried and as I afterward learned he was from Maryland, my native land, which made me value him still higher. At twilight I returned to the company, & volunteers being called for to enter Caldwell's camp by night if possible to learn his situation I started in company with another gentleman whose name I do not recollect.[49] The moon showed bright and I told him I should take the precaution to keep down the hollow untill I reached the timber on the Salado as a man on horseback could be seen for several miles so clear was the atmosphere. We had not proceeded very far before he objected to the course I had taken through precaution & insisted on my taking a more direct route which I at last consented to, telling him that I was as willing to risk the consequences as he could be. He soon proposed to return, saying he thought it dangerous & fruitless which I would not consent to. He accordingly left alone. I proceeded on, taking the precaution to lead my horse in order to see the enemy first.

As I could see much further in the open prairie, I soon succeeded in finding Dawson's battleground and took a hasty view of the dead bodies which were horribly mangled and stripped naked.[50] I took the trail again and went in search of Caldwell's company and to my joyful surprise I found the enemy had withdrawn. I found Caldwell preparing to fall back to await reinforcements. I informed him of the force under Capt. Billingsly which altered his determinations. I returned & conducted our company, which had by this time been joined by another company from Austin and Col. [James] Mayfield elected as commander of the Battalion, to Caldwell's company.[51]

Caldwell held his position until about 8 o'clock on the morning of the 20th during which time he received no further information and the enemy commenced their retreat. We pursued them with about 300 men, crossed the Medina River and encamped about 12 o'clock at night on the morning of the 21st. We crossed the river and continued up the east bank taking several prisoners & killing one of their spies. We learned that the enemy was at the upper ford and would not move until next morning. About 12 o'clock we crossed the river for the purpose of procuring an advantageous position, to rest and grase our horses. At 2 p.m. we were reinforced by 100 men. We again took the east bank of the river and marched towards the enemy, coming near them about 8 o'clock p.m. A halt was called & Capt. Hays of the spie company with several of his horsemen were sent to spie out & ascertain the position of the enemy. He returned after crossing the river & thoroughly reconnoitering the enemies' camp and reported their position favourable for an immediate attack. It was, however, deferred. At daybreak we received intelligence of another reinforcement of a hundred men which would be able to join us by 8 a.m. We waited until they came up. Our force now amounted to 500 men, and we took up the line of march in pursuit of the enemy but found they had made a hasty retreat about 1 p.m.

Capt. Hays came up with and received a few shots from the rear guard of the enemy in which Capt. Lucky [Samuel H. Luckie] was shot through the body.[52] Our field officers formed the men but instead of advancing immediately one hour was spent in useless delay, the commander affecting to believe that the attack would be made by the enemy. He at last started to the supposed position of the enemy but found they were still retreating as fast as possible. About 5 o'clock p.m. we came up with them again & Capt. Hays was ordered to bring on the engagement by an attack on the rear guard of the enemy with the assurance from Col. Mayfield & Caldwell that he should be immediately supported. Col. Caldwell instructed Col. Mayfield to select a hundred of the best mounted & equipped men in the 2nd Battalion which he commanded to support Capt. Hays in the charge. Col. Mayfield unfortunately halted the Battalion but before he could execute the order it was countermanded by an order to move on with the whole Battalion. Meanwhile Capt. Hays was ordered to make an immediate attack on their rear which was promptly executed. He succeeded in driving them from their field pieces with trifling loss, but finding he could not be supported in time by the main body he immediately fell back with two men wounded & two horses killed.

Col. Mayfield with the 2 Battalions was ordered to dismount, tie their horses, and recommence the action. Col. John H. Moore with the first Battalion was ordered to act as a horse guard & reserve, while the 2nd Battalion brought on engagement.[53] The 2nd Battalion was anxious for the conflict notwithstanding they disapproved of half our force being held back as reserve, but notwithstanding our anxiety & the earnest solicitations of Capt. Hays to make the attack, we were ordered to countermarch and fall back to our horses after we had approached nearly in rifle shot of the enemy & were only obscured from them by the musquet undergrowth on the bank of the Arroyo Hondo, a creek which did not run, though it had aplenty of large holes of good water.

About 8 o'clock p.m. we proceeded up the creek to get water, were fired on from the opposite side of the creek by the piquet guard of the enemy. The bullets whistled close to our heads without doing any damage and we proceeded on without thinking them worthy of sufficient notice to return the compliment. We encamped about $1\frac{1}{2}$ miles above the enemy, Col. Caldwell still affecting to believe he would be attacked by the enemy, but he laid down to sleep without sending out any spie to watch the movements of the enemy. Capt. Hays by his continued exertion & his company were so much fatigued and had so lost confidence in Col. Caldwell that they would not voluntarily undertake the service.

At 12 o'clock a proposition originated amongst the men for about 50 men to go down the Creek, drive in the enemies outpost & bring on a skirmish which might lead to a general engagement. Col. Caldwell could not be found in the camp to sanction the proposition. Col. Mayfield, however, took the responsibility. About 30 men arose from their slumbers to participate in this service but the majority of them deeming it rather too daring an adventure for so small a number of men to undertake, only twelve could be found willing to go. They proceeded down the creek and soon ascertained that the enemy had again retreated. This fact was communicated in camp and many of the men were up and saddling their horses.

Col. Caldwell was at length roused but still pretended to believe that he would be attacked in the morning. Col. Mayfield was now requested by several of his friends to take command and pursue the enemy as it was evident that Caldwell did not mean to fight them, but Col. Mayfield was unwilling to take this responsibility and after some time spent in useless delay the men were ordered to restake their horses and await till morning. The sun had risen on the morning of the 23rd before the men were ordered to get up, make coffee, and prepare for a start.

At 8 a.m. Battalions were formed and Col. Caldwell made a speech to justify himself in returning in which he represented the probability of the enemy being reinforced. Also stated that we had no provisions and also represented the enemy as being very superior to us and that they were commanded by an able & experienced general and he therefore thought it prudent to return. Col. Mayfield sanctioned what had been said by Caldwell and to the great disappointment of his friends also recommended that we should all return. This unexpected address from Mayfield acted like an electrick shock. One voice called out for a vote on the question but the motion was not seconded and all was silent for a half hour. When we had proceeded several miles homeward curses loud & deep were heaped upon the fickal officers and much discontent manifested. The enemies' drums had been heard at daybreak and abundance of cattle were in sight. We afterwards learned that the enemy had left the greatest portion of their baggage, their ammunition, waggons, and one piece of artillery. The officers of the enemy have since acknowledged that their men were panick struck and nothing but our own cowardise prevented us from taking them all prisoners.

On the same day we returned we were met by an express informing us that Gen. [Edward] Burleson was on his way with 200 men to join us, though it did not influence our officers to recommence the pursuit.[54] Thus a very important advantage was lost for the want of more resolute & determined officers.

On the 24th we returned to Bexar. On 25th a meeting of the

troops was called at the Alamo by General Burleson and it was recommended by him and all the officers that the troops should return home and meet again at Bexar on the 25th of October and immediately take up the line of march for the Rio Grande as this would give the people time to prepare themselves for an effective campaign. A number of men who had no business to call them home remained in the vicinity of Bexar. We next learned that Sam Houston had ordered out the 1st & 2nd Brigades of malitia which prevented Gen. Burleson from making any farther exertion to raise a force to carry on the campaign. The rivers were in the meanwhile very high which occasioned great delay.

The malitia from Montgomery County under Col. [Joseph L.] Bennett were the first who arrived in any large number though several hundred volunteers had arrived in small parties. The malitia under Bennett soon manifested a strong disposition to return home and eventually some did so after eating & destroying much of the subsistence necessary to carry on the campaign.[55] Before the troops could be organized for the campaign Sam Houston gave it as his opinion that it was unconstitutional to order the malitia across the Rio Grande. Yet Somerville was forced upon them as a commander with discretionary authority to cross the River. The volunteers had little faith in Somerville, but rather than the campaign should fall through again they cheerfully consented to go under his command by his pledging himself to cross the River.

Early in November our force amounted to about 1000 men at which time they moved westward and encamped on the Leon & Medina untill about the 28th of November at which time we took up the line of march. Our force however by unnecessary delay had decreased to about 750 men. We had been waiting for the artilery to arrive from Gonzales and after we had got it a council of war decided on changing the point of destination and leaving the field piece behind. The determination was to strike the river at Laredo, cross & proceed downward as far as prudent. On the second night we encamped at Navarros Ranch on the Tascosa.

On the 3rd day our troubles commenced. We had rain and post oak country to travel through. We had not proceeded far untill it became impossible to ride, and many of our best horses were bogged and it was with difficulty we could find firm ground enough to encamp on. We were three days in this situation, losing a number of our packs. On the 3rd day we struck the old Laredo Road and our traveling was much improved. The Nueces was high but we crossed it without much delay.[56]

Capt. Hays was sent ahead to gain information. He succeeded in catching two Mexican spies and gained all necessary information. Previous to our entering the place he informed Gen. Somerville of his success and the main body hurried on as fast as possible. As the service in which Capt. Hays had been engaged was very laborious and fatiguing to his men & horses, and supposing one of the prisoners to be severely wounded he determined to await the arrival of Gen. Somerville. But through the carelessness of [William] Alsbury who was on guard the wounded prisoner made his escape and gave information of our approach which gave the soldiers at Laredo time to make their escape or disguise themselves so that we could not distinguish them from the citizens.[57]

On the 7th of December at night Col. [James R.] Cook was sent with some picked men to procure the boats at the ford to effect a crossing with 150 men to take Col. Bravo with about 100 regular soldiers on the opposite side of the town. Two men of the spie company were sent up to find the boats with instructions to drop down below the town. They succeeded in finding a large canoe which would carry 25 men but having no paddles they concluded to let it remain where it was. As the water was much more favorable for crossing at this point than what it was below they returned & reported to Col. Cook who returned and reported to Gen. Somerville. After much time spent useless, Col. Cook was ordered to take the boat & cross 150 men before day for the purpose of taking the fort on the opposite side which was reported to be manned by 80 regulars and 20 rancheros. Col. Cook showed no disposition to perform this duty and deferred it untill it was too late.[58]

At daylight we surrounded the town & took town & the Alcalde was informed of our mission & we received possession of it without resistance. We marched & encamped about 1 league from town. The men were hungry & no grass for their horses and no assurance that their wants should be supplied by a requisition. No guard was placed to prevent the men from going to town. The consequence was that many of the men were in the town and some of them commenced plundering by taking such things as was necessary to their actual wants. The men were then informed by the officers that a requisition had been made on the town but it was now too late. Pillage had commenced and it was difficult to check it immediately. In the evening we moved our camp below town to get grazing for our horses. Here Dubois of Cameron's Co. was killed accidently.[59]

On the 9th it was ascertained that some of the men had taken articles that they were not entitled to by the rules of war. Much dissatisfaction prevailed in consequence as the great majority of the men were disposed to war with the enemy on the most magnanimous principles of civilized warfare. The captains of companies were all ordered to see that all property taken by their respective companies should be delivered up to the Quarter master which was as far as practicable complied with & the things thus taken were delivered up to the Alcalde of the town. It is due to Capt. Hays' & Cameron's companies to say they did not participate at all in this plundering.[60]

On the evening of the 9th we left Laredo and after traveling until 9 or 10 o'clock at night through a thick chapperell we encamped without water. Much discontent prevailed in consequence of not crossing the River at Laredo. About 10 o'clock on the 10th we found water and halted to grase our horses.

Gen Somerville here formed the men and asked them if they would pledge themselves not to molest any private property and be submissive to orders. All the men with the exception of 150 who returned home pledged themselves to do so.

While Somerville proceeded down the River and crossed opposite Guerrero a few troops amounting to several hundred showed themselves under Canalles, but they disappeared as soon as about 30 of our men showed themselves on the west bank. On the next morning, the 14th, we finished crossing the whole force. Commissioners came out to inform us they would surrender the town and fill any requisition we might make. They offered us quarters in the town which the officers did not choose to accept although the weather was very bad. We encamped near the town and after having our requisition partly complied with which was very insufficient, on the following day we returned to the bank of the River. Much dissatisfaction prevailed amongst the men in consequence of Somerville's not making a larger requisition and allso of his not inforcing the one he had made. On the same night our troops commenced crossing the River.

On the next morning 10 men of the spie company were sent into town to demand an immediate fulfilment of the requisition. The authorities of the town expressed a great willingness to do so but made many excuses and continued to bring in our supplies very slowly, so much so that it was evident that they intended to detain us as long as possible, so much so that it rather provoked Gen. Somerville & on the next morning Capt. Hays with his company and a part of Capt. Bryant's was ordered to town to state to the Alcalde that as he had shown no disposition to comply with the first requisition according to agreement and he therefore made a demand on them for 5000 dollars which if not complied with in a very short time that he would march his men into the town and ransack it. Capt. Hays was instructed to wait two hours and return in this time. They raised 380 dollars which Capt. Hays would not receive and returned to camp. The Alcalde however insisted on taking the money to Gen. Somerville in person, who had with the main body of his men crossed to the east bank of the River, and when he was informed of the amount of money they had raised he told him to go to hell with it. On the same night we all crossed the River. The next day Gen. Somerville ordered the flat boats sunk which were taken from Guerrero. This order, however, was not complied with as there were many of the men on foot who wanted the boats to go down the river and allso to assist us in crossing at Mier.

Gen. Somerville took up the line of march homeward with about 300 men & about 300 proceeded down the River, electing Col. Fisher as commander.[61] The boats were under the direction of Gen. Green, manned by about 60 men. The fleet consisted of four flat boats and as many canoes. Their business was to destroy all the boats which they could not take with them and procure supplies wherever practicable. We encamped together every night.

On the 22nd 8 men under [Ben] McCulloch crossed the river for the purpose of spying out the town of Mier.[62] We reconnoitered and entered the town & the Alcalde was informed of our mission and we returned to camp with information that Gen. Ampudia was hourly expected in Mier with a large force. Col. Fisher, however, crossed the River with his men the next morning, the 23rd of Dec., and marched to the town and entered without opposition. Our requisition was made out and the Alcalde expressed a willingness to comply with our requisition and commenced collecting his stores but it was evident that he intended to prolong the time as much as possible. We waited until late in the afternoon when Col. Fisher left town taking the Alcalde along to insure the fulfillment of the requisition which his inferior officers promised to deliver on the bank of the river down below our camp. ([Jesse] Yokum killed accidentally on our return). On the 26th we marched down the river to the place where the provisions was to be delivered but encamped before we reached it. ([Gideon K.] Lewis & [Allen] Holderman taken prisoner).[63]

On the 25th we learned that Gen. Ampudia & Canalles was encamped on the river below and were waiting our approach. We immediately determined on crossing the river and giving them battle, leaving about forty men to guard the horses which all did with the exception of about 15 to act as spies or scouts. Myself & both of my messmates were chosen to perform this service, Capt. Baker being in command of the scouts.

We had not proceeded far before we discovered several of their spies. Four of us immediately pursued them, depending on our horses in case of danger being ahead. I soon found myself in close gunshot of about 50 well mounted men. I brought my piece to bear upon them but finding I could have no support from my comrades, I determined to reserve my fire untill the last resort. My two messmates & one other of the scouts were all that was in sight. Of course a hasty retreat was necessary, being then close pursued by the cavalry & under a continual fire of scopits.[64] One of my messmates was taken prisoner while in the act of mounting his horse, his girt having broke which caused him to dismount. I should have made a safe retreat had not my other messmate who was ahead of me taken the wrong trail which led us into a labour surrounded by a high bulrush fence from which it was impossible to escape with our horses. We accordingly dismounted, my two companions making their escape by climbing over the brush fence which I might have done allso had I not been too anxious to give them a shot. When I raised my gun they were in thirty feet of me. I then discovered I had lost both caps of my gun and before I could recap it a half dozen of them had seized me. They tied my arms. One of them took me behind him and hurried me off to town.[65] I was taken before Gen. Ampudia who informed me that I must tell him the truth. If not he would have me shot. I replied to him that his threats would make no difference in my answers to him, that I was his prisoner and he could dispose of me as he thought proper.

I was asked by the interpreter if I was not a spie. I told him I was a scout, but he insisted otherwise while I stated that a spie was one who tried to obtain important information by palming himself on the enemy as a friend. Nothing more was said on that subject.

I was now asked many questions relative to Col. Fisher's movements & intentions, about Gen. Rusk & Burleson divisions and allso Gen. Somerville. To all of these questions I gave evasive replies except as regarded the disposition of our men to fight to which I told him they had been waiting for some time to get a fight and were not willing to go home without it—that they were resolved on death or victory. I now discovered my messmate who had been taken and we were both conducted to a small prison joining the Alcalde's office where we found Lewis & Holderman who had been taken the day before. We were locked up and before we had finished relating each others adventures heard a volley of musquetry which was answered by a volley of rifles. The bullets whistled about our door. The sentinels departed their post and ran in the house but soon returned, and tied us so tight with our arms behind us that we were in much pain, not forgetting to rifle our pockets for the small change. The guard deserted this place and retreated to the opposite side of the square. The fire of musquetry & cannon was kept up all night without intermission, with an occasional report from a rifle. We waited with much anxiety till daylight, when the dread sound of the rifles silenced many of the muskets and at length silenced many of the artillery. The officers had their horses saddled, servants holding them near the gate of the back yard, open evidently for the purpose of retreating. At 2 or 3 p.m. the firing ceased. [D. H. E.] Beasley, [Richard] Keene & Dr. Senicson [John J. Sinnickson] were brought in as prisoners, and we were soon informed by Gen. Ampudia that Gen. Fisher & Green had surrendered to him.[66] We were then untied and in a short time joined our unfortunate companions who had been induced to surrender as prisoners of war. From them we learned that the entering of the town on the part of Green & Fisher was a very gallant affair, but after Col. Fisher became satisfied of the force he had to contend with which amounted to about 3000 men, he became low spirited and gave his men no encouragement, but on the contrary when a white flag was brought in by Dock Sinecson (who had been left a short distance from town with 10 men to take care of [Joseph] Berry who had his leg broke by a fall on the rocks and was taken prisoner) it is said that Fisher showed a great want of firmness and after holding an interview with the enemy, he returned to his men with representations well calculated to cause a division in our ranks, telling the men that he was acquainted with Col. Huiras [?] and knew him to be a gentleman of his word, and he had such & such assurances from him which the men might rely upon. He then told his men that all who was in favour of surrendering should march to the public square and surrender their arms. This created great confusion and resulted in the surrender of the whole. Our loss was 11 killed and 22 wounded; 263 men crossed the river; about 40 odd were left as campguard with the horses. Chalk & Sinclair made their escape from Mier by concealing themselves in a bake oven at night. Bascus [Vásquez] allso made his escape.[67] The loss of the enemy was between 6 and 700 killed or wounded, the most of the wounds being fatal as the Texians had nothing to shoot at but their heads as they stuck them above the ramparts on the houses.

On the morning of the 27 of December a guard with several of
our men were sent out to cross the river to inform our camp guard
of our surrender and to demand the same of them, but to our great
joy we learned that they would not surrender. On the 28 a large
force of cavalry pursued them but we were happy to see them return without success. The guard sent to camp to get our camp
equipage, blankets, etc., left nearly everything of any value so that
many of the men were left entirely without covering and suffered
much in consequence.

On the 31st started for Matamoras. Marched 5 leagues to Camargo. Encamped for the night in the suburbs of the town having
left 23 men in Mier, 21 wounded, one to act as interpreter. Sunday, 1st January, 1843 crossed the St. John [San Juan] River &
entered the town of Camargo amidst a great parade & triumph of
the citizens displaying handkerchiefs & banners to the honour &
glory of Canalles and Ampudia. We remained in quartells untill
the 2nd. Marched 10 miles and encamped at a rancho, herded in a
cowpen.

Tuesday, 3rd. Made an early start marching 21 miles over a
much better section of country than any we had yet seen and encamped at Old Reinosa in a sheep pen.

Wednesday, 4th. Took up the line of march for New Reinosa,
18 miles distant. We arrived at foot of the hill on which the town
was situated about 2 o'clock p.m. and halted a short time and
ordered to march two & two. As we approached the firing of guns
commenced and lasted for an hour while we were marched under
a great many triumphal arches which were decorated by the shawls
and kerchiefs & petticoats of the ladies. As we entered the square
about thirty children dressed in fantastic stile were dancing to the
music of the bells. We were gazed on by the inhabitants with great
astonishment. Their much triumph affected the feelings of our
men very differently. Some of them laughed at their insignificance;
others would occasionally give a yell as the muskats & firecrackers

went off, while others again would scarcely contain themselves with indignation and rage. After the parade was over we were marched to a large unfurnished brick building where we remained untill the 6th. (Left [Samuel] McDade sick.)[68]

Marched to church to witness the ceremony of mass which was completed by firing of cannon & we marched 25 miles after late start. Encamped in a corral.

Saturday, 7th. Marched 18 miles and encamped in a corral for the night.

Sunday, 8th. Marched 13 miles over a low musquet country and some prairie admirably adapted to the cultivation of sugar though there is not a great deal cultivated. We encamped at a large ranch called Warloupe [Guadalupe]. On Monday, 9th, we started early for Matamoras 3 leagues distant. There the Mexicans endeavoured to make as grand a display as possible. The road for some distance out of town was crowded with men, women & children to greet their husbands & sweethearts, but many of them were disappointed as their sweethearts & husbands had experienced the effects of Texian Rifles at Mier. The main avenue leading to the square was decorated with triumphal arches and crowded with all sects, sizes, & colours, some of them hissing at us as we passed. We saw a good many foreigners who appeared much interested in our situation. We were much admired for our bravery by some of the Mexican officers. Our comforts were greatly increased by the donations of clothing and blankets sent in to our prison by the foreigners, and our thanks & gratitude is particularly due to Mr. Marks, the U.S. consul and a Mr. J. P. Schatzell who advanced a large sum to different individuals. He formerly resided in Kentucky.[69] Here we had the privilege of writing home and some of the men embraced this opportunity.

A consultation was held by the Mexican officers relative to our being ironed which was, so we learned, strongly insisted upon by Canalles, stating that he would not guard us without. This was protested against by Fisher & Green, & Gen. Ampudia at length decided that we should not be ironed but determined on sending our staff officers ahead of us as a precautionary measure to prevent us from attempting our escape, being told that if any attempt was made they would be held responsible.

On the 12th, Green, Fisher, Murray [Thomas A. Murry], Shepperd [Dr. William M. Shepherd], Capt. Lions [Samuel C. Lyon], & D. Henry [Daniel Drake Henrie], interpreter, left for Mexico City via Monterey [Monterrey].[70]

Sat., 14th. We left Matamoras for Mexico via Monterey, Saltillo & San Louis [Luis] Potosi. We marched 12 miles & encamped for the night. Our guard was about 500 with one piece of artillery commanded by Canalles. We did not have strong hopes of whipping our guard and making our escape home.

Sunday, 15th. Marched 20 miles over a tolerably good country. Light rain and disagreeable traveling.

Monday, 16th. Marched 20 miles and encamped in a corral or in English, a cowpen.

Tuesday, 17th. Marched 24 miles & encamped in a corral.

18th. Marched early, Watered at 18 miles in a pool or artificial lake which are common in Mexico. At 25 miles we encamped for the night in a corral at a stone ranch.

19th. Marched 12 miles and encamped in a corral at a large ranch Lacoma.

20th. Marched 18 miles and encamped for the night. Here we intended to attack the guards but were suspected and thought it prudent to defer it till a more favourable opportunity.

21st. Marched 20 miles to a small village on the St. John called the Pass Suarte and encamped in a corral for the night. We were now almost unanimous in favour of making the attack. Cameron being the oldest and most experienced captain was unanimously chosen as commander. He was to designate the point of attack for each captain and to give the word in such a manner as to attract no suspicion. To effect this it was necessary to wait until we were ordered to form for the purpose of drawing our rations. The cannon was placed in front of the bars & Dr. [Richard F.] Brenham was instructed to choose 25 men to take possession of it.[71] The capts. had their duties assigned them and we were all formed ready for the attack. The bars however, were up and two men stood ready to draw them out to enable us to get out as quick as possible. The commissary was allso ready to issue his rations of flour. The commander gave the word to draw away, meaning to draw away the bars, but this was misunderstood as the order to draw provisions. A moments consideration and a suggestion from Capt. Baker that it would be better to wait until we got in the mountains when we would have less guard and a more favourable country to retreat over changed his mind and the question was not again to be agitated until we left Monterey.[72] This determination myself & many others were opposed to, though we could not help it as it was important that we should all be united in such an undertaking. From this place we could have crossed the Rio Grande in about 16 hours and made our escape without doubt.

Sunday, 22nd. Crossed the river St. John & marched twelve miles & encamped at Palmetto Ranch. We were put in a stone fort made as a barrier against the Comanches.

23rd. Marched. Passed a large ranch at 3 miles. At 12 miles at 12 o'clock came to a village called Mantaca. Encamped in a corral.

24th. Marched 24 miles, crossing a small creek early in the morning and encamped in a corral.

25th. At 5 miles came to Capisaro on the river of the same name, a branch of the St. John. Crossed the river and inclined upward the mountains. Crossed a creek at 21 miles. Encamped in a corral for the night.

26th. Marched 15 miles to Padaset, crossed a small stream close to the town. This is a pretty place of about 5000 inhabitants in a very pretty little valley. As usual we were marched in triumph under triumphal arches.

27th. Moved to a better situation. Friend Bullock gave us tobacco.[73]

28th. Saturday. Bad roads from a great deal of rain. Marched for Monteray and encamped at 15 miles to a large rancho. There is several sugar farms in this neighborhood. The land is so situated as to be irrigated by the river.

Sunday, 29th. Marched. At 6 miles passed Warloupe [Guadalupe] Mission. At 9 miles came to Monteray the first city of the mountains and in the state of New Leon. Monteray is situated between 2 mountains and on a branch of the San Whon [Juan]. The highest peak is called the Comanche Saddle and is about 1500 feet. Less parade over us here than elsewhere.

Monday, 30th; Tuesday, 31st; February 1st. Remained in prison at this place.

February 2 at 2 o'clock left Monteray for Saltillo and encamped at a ranch 12 miles distant, San Catherine.

3rd. Marched 24 miles to a large Ranch Rinconada. Here we intended to attack the guard, take their arms and make our escape to Texas, the guard as we anticipated having been much reduced. But they received some warning which put them on their guard which prevented it. We supposed that Capt. [Charles K.] Reese had informed the Commander.[74]

4th. Marched 27 miles and camped. Our course due west inclining up the river or valley of Monterey between two rugged ledges of mountains.

Sunday, 5th. Marched 12 miles to the city of Saltillo. This town is situated on the waters of the River St. John in a pretty little valley surrounded by rocky, dreary looking mountains without vegetation.

6th. Remained in prison. We here overtook our officers and 5 of

Woll's prisoners, amongst them was [George] Van Ness, who was taken as interpreter to go on with our officers who continued to go ahead of us.[75] Here we secured a donation of tobacco from a liberal Frenchman.

7th. Took up the line of march for San Louis Potosi. Marched 24 miles & camped at the ranch where [Philip] Dimmit's men made their escape from the guard, and Dimmit killed himself by poison to prevent being killed by the enemy who treated him very brutally.[76] The name of the ranch is Agua Nuevo which is in English New Water.

Wednesday, 8th. Marched 24 miles and came to water at a tank or artificial lake. At 12 miles farther encamped at a large ranch called San Salvadore. The water was very brackish being drawn from a deep well by means of a wheel worked by a mule with buckets on a large belt in which the water is drawn up.

Thursday, 9th. Marched 33 miles to a large ranch and camped in a corral. Here the water is allso brackish and the country very poor & barren, almost destitute of vegitation.

Friday, 10th. Marched 20 miles and encamped at a large ranch called the Salado. Here we again overtook our officers and had some little intercourse with them. They did not advise us much in regard to our attack on the guard but told us to use our own judgement.

We had been arguing & agitating the subject for some time, but could not get the men unanimous although more favourable opportunities had passed than the present both for attack and retreat. But the men appeared now to be more desperate and determined at all hazards to strike a blow which might once more regain their liberty. Col. Barragan's treatment to us had not been very harsh untill the last two days when his conduct bid fain to be rather cruel toward us for the future as he had given the soldiers liberty to whip us and several of our men had already experienced their cruelty. It now appeared from the report of the captains that a majority of the men was in favour of making an attempt to regain our liberty. The next morning was agreed upon for the attack.

It was agreed that the signal should be given when the commander came into the yard to order us up to draw our rations and prepare for the march as was his usual custom. He came in early in the morning, discovered our excitement, & retired immediately before the word was given, but notwithstanding this important advantage of taking the commander was lost, there were some who were yet determined and urged the attack with a great deal of zeal. It now appeared to be the last chance and many of us were determined not to let it pass. Our commander after much persuasion gave the word of attack in a very cool & deliberate manner by pulling off his hat, telling his men to come on and taking the musket from the sentinell on the left of the door while I took the one on the right.

The rush was now as great as the size of the door would admit of. About 150 infantry were stationed in the yard adjoining the one we were in. And notwithstanding the warning they had of our intention to attack and the precaution to prevent it, we had full possession of the yard in about 5 minutes and the soldiers begging for quarters which was readily granted, not killing any more of them than was actually necessary to receive their arms from them. Some of them still kept a brisk fire. Here [Archibald] Fitzgerald was mortally wounded. We charged up to the door of the yard to which they had retired where we exchanged a number of shots and John Stansbury was shot in the eye while in the act of firing his piece. The orders was now given to cease firing.[77]

I was now on the opposite side of the door where Stansbury was shot, and endeavoured to make the Mexicans cease firing also by calling to them in their own language, but the soldier who had shot Stansbury as if he was elated with success continued to load without seeming to notice me atall. I took a deliberate aim and the gentleman tumbled from his position without ceremony. I now discovered by the whizing of the balls that we were exposed to a cross fire from some port holes in an offset in the corner of the wall for defence against the Indians. Myself and one of my comrades ran down to it and jabing a rock in the hole the firing intirely ceased. About 40 or 50 of the cavalry with the Commander made their escape. All the rest fell into our hands as prisoners though we did not detain them or exact any conditions of them nor take anything but what we were entitled to by the rules of war. We got about 70 horses & mules & saddles, about 1400 dollars of public money, ammunition, provisions, arms, etc.

Our officers, [who] had been marched off about 15 minutes before the action commenced under the charge of Capt. Romano, were halted when the firing commenced and when halted Capt. Romano received an order from Col. Barrogan to execute them. They replied to him that they were at his disposal. He told them they were in the hands of a gentleman and in a short time ordered them to mount and I have since learned traveled through 75 miles without resting only sufficient time to get fresh horses.[78] In the action we had two men, [Richard F.] Brenham & Lions [Patrick Lyons], a Scotchman, killed dead; one man by the name of [Lorenzo] Rice killed dead in the horse trough in the yard where we slept & two others mortally wounded, since dead, [Archibald] Fitzgerald & Haggerty & five others, [J. R.] Baker and [George] W. Trahern & Stansbury severely wounded; [Thomas] Hancock & [John] Harvey slightly wounded, the latter being wounded in the yard where we slept while not taking any part in the action.[79] We were very unfortunate in losing Fitzgerald & allso Hancock who was too much affected at the time to go with us supposing a stab which he received to have reached the hollow, though it proved otherwise. On these two men we depended as guides as they had a better knowledge of the country over which we intended to pass than anyone else we had along.

Before proceeding farther, I must stop to make some remarks

about Capt. [Charles K.] Reese whose conduct has been censured by his comrades. In the first place, he is said to have acted childish at Mier when the white flag was brought in by Doct. Senicson, crying & telling him he had saved his life. In the next place he is guilty of inconsistency such as advocating an attack on the guard on our way to Matamoros while our guard was five to one, and, while on our march to Monterey with a much less guard and everyone entertaining hopes of escape, he went so far as to bribe the guard to let him escape but had not sufficient nerve to go after he succeeded in getting the consent of the soldiers who guarded him when he went after water.

At Monterey he again intended to make his escape if he could have persuaded others to have gone with him, notwithstanding he knew there would be opportunity of all of us making our escape and we all felt confident of the same and an attempt by him to escape would have been a great barrier to our success; and on the second night from Monterey when we had positively determined on the attack he now disapproved of the attack although we could have reached the Rio Grande in three days and not have lost a man in the attack; and besides he was engaged in conversation with the commander early in the morning, the infantry was put under arms much earlier than usual and prevented the attack from being made in the course of the day. One of our Lieutenants, [John] Shipman, was informed of our intentions.[80] We have since judged that it was Capt. Reese gave information.

Capt. Reese was now opposed to our break and continued in the confidence of Barragan and was treated with much more attention than any other officers amongst us. When we arrived at the Salado, Capt. Reese was angry with those who advocated an attack and made himself noisy & clamorous in opposing it. At night he was out in company with Barragan and again the guard was doubled and precautionary measures taken to prevent it. Capt. Reese declared he would take no part in it and persuaded a number of others to remain neutral. After the fight was over he came out and made preparation to go with us but determined to send his brother, William Reese, with Barragan to Mexico. After we had spent about two hours in preparing to march and several of our interpreters had conversed with Barragan in which they learned from him that Capt. Reese had told him that he thought he could prevent an attack, and after being mounted on a good horse & musket which himself & Brother both secured he went over with it as a peace offering to the enemy and never more returned to us.[81] It is due however to say for the credit of Wm. Reese that he fought bravely although his brother forbid him.

In relation to the 1st charge however it is confuted by Doct. Sinicson who clears him of any want of manly behaviour in the affair at Mier. Dr. Sinicson however is liable to answer and perhaps very justly so as he has since acknowledged that it was his opinion that the enemy was whipped when he came in with the white flag and did not express his opinion to the Texians which would in all probability have made the most timid willing to have fought on instead of surrendering. His reason for not doing so is that some unforeseen event might have changed the anticipated assault or rather might possibly have given the battle in favour of the Mexicans and in that event the Texians all put to the sword as the Mexican officers threatened in case they did not surrender which he says might have been a charge of infamy against him hereafter by making representations which were not.

But I must now return to the Salado. About 10 o'clock we took up the line of march homeward.[82] Including the wounded & sick, we left 18 men at the Salado. We marched 53 miles and stopped again at San Salvadore and bought corn & fed our horses & proceeded on. At 65 miles slept about two hours before day. We were dogged behind by the cavalry that escaped at the Salado though they manifested little disposition to come very close to us.

Sunday, 12th. Marched early in the morning. Leaving the Saltillo Road at 10 o'clock, struck the Zacatecas Road at about 10 miles and took the left hand to a ranch in sight for the purpose of obtaining water. We found the tank was close to the house which was defended by a few regular troops who hoisted a red flag and commenced a fire on us at about 200 yards. Our commander determined not to be detained by any argument that he could avoid. Our men however showed great coolness. As they filed right they marched deliberately off under the fire of the fort while the bullets were whizing about our heads, no other man as I did even dodging his head except the Reverend Parson [Thomas W.] Cox.[83] We had no damage, only a horse wounded.

We directed our course northward to a trail we discovered leading over the mountain which was very rough in ascending. However, we were fortunate enough to find a hole of water, the greatest treat we could have had at this time being about 20 hours without any. It was truly a godsend and just about as much as would give us a drink around. Here we discovered a party of Mexicans dogging us, and the two Sargeants left us and went to Saltillo.[84] Proceeded on. At about 6 miles came to a ranch where we got water for our horses. We found them in arms but did not molest them except to inquire the Camargo Road and proceeded on without any intention however of taking it but more for the purpose of deceiving them than otherwise about the road we intended to take. We continued our course west and after descending a mountain into a deep valley about 3 o'clock at night we laid down to rest placing a guard out, and took a Mexican spie who rode into our camp. Here Jack Sweizy was left asleep or deserted us.[85]

Monday, February 13th. We started early taking the prisoner with us, our course west. At 8 miles came to water and proceeded on and struck the Montclova Road. Here a friend came to us and gave us directions & advice which we ought to have followed but for want of confidence in him we did not do so. The prisoner we had taken was to act as pilot. At 12 o'clock crossed a small creek and came to a ranch and sent John Brennan, the interpreter, and our Mexican to buy some corn & beef.[86] The Mexican was detained and John Brennan told to leave or he would be fired on. We passed in gunshot of the ranch not molesting anything. A woman then came out and inquired if any of Jordan's men was with us and being told there was she said if they would vouch for the good behaviour of the rest that we could be accomodated at the ranch with what we wanted.[87] We would not return though and continued our course and was soon overtaken by the proprietor of the ranch who expressed some regret that we had been mistaken in our intentions and showed us a good place some short distance from the ranch to graze and rest our horses. At sunset we again took up the line of march and left the road at 8 o'clock to sleep. Were fired on by a small party of Mexicans. We then proceeded on.

Our commander was now influenced to leave the road entirely and take the mountains contrary to his instructions and his own judgement, and, as well as I can learn, influenced by officers and men who attached much of prudence as being the better part of valour and opposed the break at the Salado and done little towards fighting out after it was begun. We continued our march five miles & encamped for the night placing out a guard.

February 14th. Directed our course through the mountains. Traveled hard and made but little progress. The country too rough for our horses. Found no water. Being much fatigued encamped for the night in a very deep ravine having passed a shepperd with a large flock of sheep in the morning and allso learned that we would find no water the direction we were going which ought to have been sufficient warning to have induced us to return to the road.

15th. Some of our men found water about a mile & a half from camp. We now determined on leaving our horses and taking it on

Texians killing their horses in the mountains for sustenance.

Charles McLaughlin, a participant, drew this and the three sketches that follow. McLaughlin's sketches first appeared in Green's *Journal of the Texian Expedition Against Mier.*

foot. We proceeded to kill the fattest and best of our horses & mules & jerk the meat for our subsistence and cut up the saddle flaps to make sandals to protect our feet from the rock & thorns. The scene here was awfully grand, so much so that language cannot fully describe it. It presented a map of destruction and a set of men reduced to the necessity of eating mules & horse flesh apparently in fine spirits & willing to endure any hardships & make any sacrifice to regain their liberty. At 3 o'clock we proceeded on, our water having given out so that the men could not fill their gourds. At 10 o'clock encamped for the night in a deep ravine having left Este, Fitzgerald, & Isam & several others that joined us in the morning before we started.[88]

16th. Continued our course north. No water, leaving Miller & Pilly [Robert Michael Pilley] at camp. At 12 o'clock left Parson [Cox] and Miller & Davis who gave out & could not keep up.[89] Came to a road or trail on our course and continued on it till night. At about 14 miles farther we encamped for the night. No water. We had begun to use the palmetto as a substitute for water.

Friday, 17th. Marched early in the morning. Our course west of north at about 8 miles. Mark Rogers is unable to keep up. Holderman and Williams remained with him; about 2 o'clock discovered some Mexican spies in a large valley. Our course now northward across it. Rogers, Holderman, & Williams again overtake us while stopping to rest.[90] We proceeded and encamped about 9 o'clock without water. A number of the men, however, continued on changing their course eastward in search of water.

Saturday, 18th. No signal from any of our water hunters. Continued our course across the valley. Much dissatisfaction prevailed in regard to the course we were most likely to find water. Some were for going east and some west and some for continuing our course north thinking we might find water in the next valley. The men, however, were all unable to travel and halted to rest. Capt. Cameron with about 50 men continued on a short distance, bearing more to the west and allso stopped to rest during the heat of the day being yet undetermined what course to take. Several small parties having already left in search of water and the main body scattered for several miles over the valley with their blankets spread on the thorn bushes to protect them from the sun. The groans of the men were now distressing even to those of the greatest fortitude and perseverance. Some of them had been drinking their urine several days. Some of them eating or chewing nigro-head & prickley pear to raise the moisture in their mouths while others were scratching up the cold dirt & gravel from the shade of the bushes and applying it to their breast & stomachs to cool their fevers.

At 6 o'clock p.m. discovered a large smoke to the right. At first supposed it to be a signal made by some of our water hunters who had gone in that direction. Sent a messenger to Col. Cameron to inform him. A large number of the men threw down their muskets unable to carry them farther and late in the evening started for the smoke. It was now impossible to keep 20 men together as some would stop to get juice from the magaya and others compelled to stop every 15 or 20 minutes to rest.

I was with a party of ten men when we came close enough to the fire to ascertain that it was a camp of Mexican cavalry. It was now about 8 o'clock at night. We passed them and continued on to where we expected water. Found several small parties had preceded us at several leagues. We passed another camp leaving it to our right and continuing in the trail that the horsemen had made leading to a large gap or pass in the mountain. At day break we came close to the top and heard a sentinel hail which proved to be one of the parties who had preceded us. Our party scattered and my friend & messmate John McMullin [McMullen] continued in company with me.[91] Bearing a little to the right and still approaching the pass we stopped a short time after, perceiving the pass was guarded, and rested at the same time consulting on what course we should pursue.

We concluded that the only alternative was surrender. We could not survive longer without water. We had one musket between us and we throwed that away and walked into camp and were met by some of the rancheros who told us to give them our money and they would take care of it for us, that if we did not the regulars would take it from us. This, however, I did not do as I had already taken the precaution to hide what little I had in the waist band of my pantaloons, knowing well that the first thing a Mexican thought of when they took a prisoner was to rob him of all he had and allso that if I gave it up I should not see it again.

In a few minutes another party of our men were brought in and a few had allso preceded us. There was now about 50 in camp and continued to come in two or three together all day. The Mexicans seemed to have some pity for us and used great precaution in giving us water or in all probability a number of the men would have killed themselves had they been allowed free access to drink what they wanted. In the evening Capt. Cameron with about 60 men were brought in having the most of them surrendered the night before at the first camp of Mexicans on the condition they should be treated as prisoners of war. We were all tied two & two with rawhide strings and the officers separated from us. This being the 19th we remained here untill the 22nd and took up the line of march for Saltillo, 134 of us in number having surrendered. They gave us plenty of raw beef & corn but very little wood to cook it and being tied so that we could only use one hand it was very troublesome to do our cooking.

On the 23rd, being the second day from the pass in the mountain came to a ranch where we found Dr. [William F.] McMath, Holderman & Towny [John Tanney].[92] On the 24th, 25th, remained at the ranch. During the time about 21 more of our men were brought in. The nights were very cold and many of the men suffered a great deal as they were nearly naked and the Mexicans had taken the blankets from them. They allso took all the money from them they could find so that many of them were left entirely destitute of almost everything.

On Sunday, 26th, marched 20 miles and encamped at a ranch in a cowpen, our number 160. Some of the sick were permitted to ride burrors or jackasses.

27th. Some of our boys were struck several times for untieing

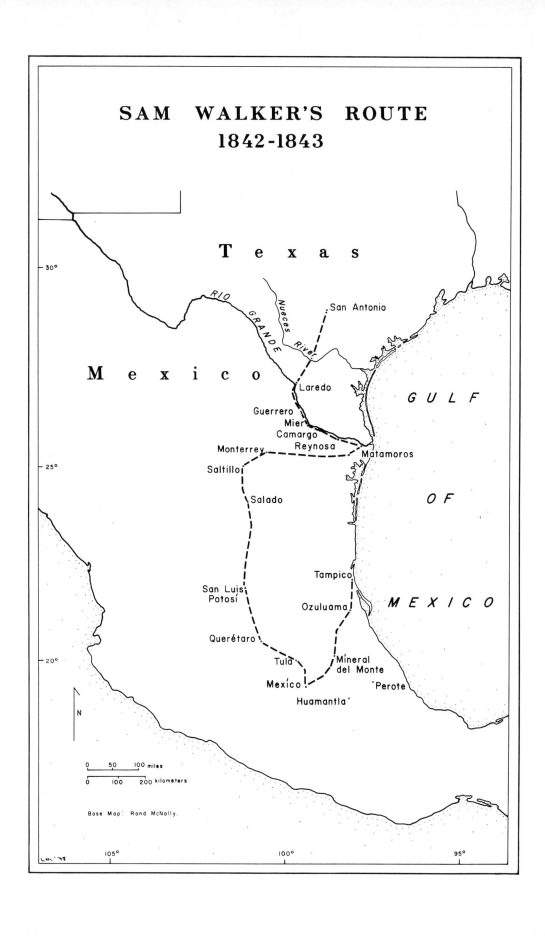

SAM WALKER'S ROUTE
1842-1843

the rawhide strings and several threatened if they done so again. Marched 24 miles and encamped at San Antonios Ranch. Here the rawhides were exchanged for handcuffs of iron. They continued to guard us very closely, not allowing us to stand up in camp lest we might charge them. Our boys however seemed determined to bear up and keep a stiff upper lip under all circumstances and on this occasion were more lively than usual, receiving their irons with smiles and promising to remunerate the Mexicans for their kindness the first opportunity. The evenings ceremony was followed by singing and telling stories which attracted the attention of the officers and ladies about the ranch who were as much amused as astonished at the unusual fortitude of our men under such circumstances.

28th. Marched 20 miles and encamped at an old camping ground. Bad water.

March 1st. Started early for the town, 16 miles. Got no water untill we reached the suburbs of the town where we were permitted for the first time to wash our faces which were thickly covered with dirt. We were then halted and remained for several hours waiting for the governor and allso for preparations to receive him which were making in the city. We entered the city with a band of music with a great parade and firing of crackers. We were marched to the square where a speech was delivered with loud cheers. We at length marched to our quarters which were very lousy. This day we get nothing to eat.

March 2nd. Got breakfast at 10 o'clock.

3rd. [Robert G.] Waters & Torry [James N. Torrey] were brought in and ironed and allso the two Sargeants who had been in town for several days.[93]

Saturday, 4th. Remained in prison.

Sunday, 5th. 9 more of our boys were brought in. Sweizy had allso been brought in.

Monday, 6th. Received a donation of tobacco from a citizen which was very thankfully received.

7th. Remained in prison.

8th. Pete Ackerman was brought in having got within 60 miles of Rio Grande before he was taken.[94]

9th. Petitioned to the governor for more rations and in addition to the one meal a day we got coffee in the evening. Brian [W. Barney C. Bryan] died from the effects of cold contracted from sleeping without a blanket. He was a young man of amiable modest unassuming disposition and a good soldier.[95]

10th and 11th. Nothing important except a comet had been discovered some nights ago which excited considerable uneasiness among the Mexicans.

11th. Nothing of importance occurred.

Sunday, 12th. Visited by some Americans who were watched closely and not allowed to converse with us. The object of their visit we did not learn but some of the men were inclined to believe they were merely desirous of knowing our condition as they expressed great surprise at seeing so many American prisoners.

There were five of the sick baptised by a Catholic priest and were afterward treated with considerable attention by some of the citizens, though we did not give them much praise for their Christianity as they visited Brian a few days previous to his death and because he would not consent to be baptised they refused to do anything for him when good attention might have saved his life. Those who were baptised were considerably censured by some of their comrades.[96]

In the meanwhile learned that an order had been sent to shoot every 10th man for the break at the Salado, but the citizens & Governor had refused to execute the order and petitions were sent to procure our release which they hoped would be granted as they agreed that our conduct at the Salado was magnanimous & brave and allso our retreat, and when they learned all the particulars that they could our commander, Capt. Cameron, was treated with more than usual kindness by Mexicans declaring they loved him and admired him for his bravery & magnanimity.

Monday, 13th, 14th, 15th, 16th, 17th. Nothing of importance occurred.

Saturday, 18th. Joe Watkins & [E. D.] Wright were brought in, found near Montclova having laid down to die for want of water. They were taken to a little town called Quarto Sinicas where they were very kindly treated after being first robbed of everything they had. They informed us of the death of [A. J.] Lewis of Brazoria, who died for want of water. They allso learned that two of our men had passed Montclova and would probably reach Texas.[97]

On the 19th and 20th an examination of our interpreters took place in relation to the break at the Salado. It was for the purpose of finding the ring leaders and the particulars allso of Col. Barragan's conduct in the action.[98]

On the 21st the cavalry arrived from San Luis Potosi to guard us on our way to the city of Mexico.

On the 22nd took up the line of march under command of Col. Orteese [Juan Ortiz] accompanied by a company of infantry. We marched 8 leagues to New Water Ranch.

23rd. Marched 14 leagues and encamped at San Salvadore Ranch. There our handcuffs were examined and all the sick men who had been loose were again ironed. We began to suspect that something was wrong yet we hoped otherwise.

24th. Marched 11 leagues and encamped for the night.

25th. Marched early and arrived at the Salado about 2 o'clock, 20 miles. Soon after we arrived we received the melancholy intelligence that every 10th man was to be shot. We were ordered to form the officers in front when the following order was read. That for the offence committed at that place on the 11th of February, the supreme government of Mexico had decreed that every 10th

Texians drawing the black beans at Salado.
  McLaughlin pictures Ewen Cameron drawing the first bean.

man should be shot. We were ironed and of course bound to sub-
mit as we could not make effectual resistance. We at once determined to bear it like men & soldiers. Had we have known it or
anticipated it we should have made another attack on the guard at
Satillo, but it is now too late. We are all closely ironed two together and the soldiers with their guns presented. The only way

we could show our bravery was to bear it with resignation & fortitude.

Our fate was decided by drawing beans from a covered mug. A white bean signified exemption from the execution, a black bean Death. The number to be executed was 17. The scene now is one of awful grandeur which surpasses description. A manly gloom and a look of firmness prevaded the countenances of all the Texians and it was difficult to distinguish by their countenances while the drawing was going on who had drawn the black beans, while some of the Mexican officers who were present shed tears as though they were much grieved to witness such a scene of horror and a disgrace to their country. The names of those unfortunate men are as follows: Capt. Wm. Eastland, T. L. Jones, Jas. M. Ogden, John S. Cash, Patrick Mahan, Henry N. Whaling, Robert Dunham, Wm. Rowan, James D. Cook [Cocke], Robert Harris, James N. Torry, J. N. M. Thompson, C. M. Roberts, James Turnbull, E. Esty [Este], M. C. Wing, Jas. L. Shepherd, the latter could not be found on the morning after the massacre.[99]

They all died with more than usual firmness, telling us in their farewell embraces that they desired their murder to be remembered and revenged by their countrymen, and some of them allso telling the Mexican officers that it was coldblooded murder and their countries should revenge their death and as small a matter as the Mexicans may think it the blood of these men may yet cost them the blood of thousands as circumstances will make it more lasting than the massacre of Fannin, which will be remembered by future generations.[100]

The deed was a dark one and needed the shades of night to execute it in. The victims after writing a few hasty lines and making some requests of their friends, were blindfolded, their hands tied behind them, and led out just at dusk, divided in two parties. A wall of 10 or 12 feet in height obscured them from our vision ex-

Shooting of the decimated Texians at Salado.
   The roster of Mier men identifies McLaughlin as a draftsman.

cept those who were permitted to see it, and very few had any
desire to witness it. The firing commenced and lasted about 5 minutes. When the groans of the murdered ceased, having shot some
of them 10 or 15 times and that in the most brutal manner, shooting their heads and faces instead of shooting them dead through
the hearts as some of them requested. At an interval of 10 or 15
minutes the firing commenced and ceased in about 5 minutes as
before. Several very little officers who came in and asked a number

of our men if we were contented. This I thought a strange question to ask men in our situation.

26th. Took a passing look at our murdered comrades who were laying pelmel as they had fallen. We marched 7 leagues and encamped in a corral. The water here is good, the first in four days.

27th. Marched 6 leagues and came to a ranch where there was a beautiful spring of running water, the first running water we found in 45 leagues, the few ranchos on the road being supplied by wells, as I have already described. The country from here to Saltillo is very poor and would afford very little supplies for an army. These wells might allso be filled up and easily destroyed by a retiring force. At 2 leagues farther we encamped at the St. John Hacienda.

28th. Four of our men were baptised. [J. P.] Wyatt, [Richard] Brown, Miller & Isam.[101] After the ceremony we marched 18 miles and camped for the night at San Christopher for the night. Here the country is more thickly settled & though very poor the inhabitants seem to have on hand a surplus of provender and provisions sufficient to feed an army.

Wednesday, 29th. Marched 30 miles and encamped at a large Hacienda Waloupa having passed several large haciendas on the road.

30th. Marched 20 miles to Lagoona Saco, a large ranch owned by a Frenchman who divided his wardrobe with us, giving us shirts etc. which we stood very much in need of. Samuel McClellan [McClelland] died here from the effects of plurisy.[102]

31st. Marched 15 miles. Watered at a large tank. Here a mule throwed Wilson.[103] At 30 miles came to the Banao, a small town on a small branch and camped for the night.

April 1st. Here we rested and was permitted to go a bathing though many of them could not get their shirts off on account of our handcuffs. This is a small place, apparently about 100 acres or

200 acres of fertile land thickly covered with fruit trees and vegetation of various descriptions surrounded by barren hills covered with rock. Yet there is a population of several thousand souls. The most remarkable growth I have ever seen for hedging or fencing is the orange which grows here in great abundance. The prickly pear allso grows to most incredible height, from 12 to 15 feet in height.

Sunday, 2nd. Again took up the line of march. Came to a small town called Gededianda and camped for the night. This is something like the Banao.

3rd. Marched 20 miles and came to another small town Laboca and camped for the night.

4th. Received a donation of cigars from the ladies of the town. Marched 20 miles and camped.

5th. Marched 5 leagues into San Louis Potosi. Marched through the public square which presented a very respectable appearance and from thence to our quarters. Here we found Capt. Baker, Stansbury, [Norman B.] Woods, & [Thomas] Colville who had been left in the hospital.[104]

6th. The handcuffs were taken off.

7th. 14 men were taken to the hospital.

8th. E. G. Caughman [Kaufman] & Robert Beard died in the hospital.[105] Here we were better fed than usual.

9th. Remained in prison.

10th. We were told here that Fisher had sold us at Mier and received a part of the money in San Louis. Did not credit the report. Were treated with great coolness by the most of the foreigners in consequence of false reports which had been circulated about us. A German merchant however was very generous & kind to our officers and some of the men, giving them clothes etc. On the 9th remained in prison. Nothing important occurred. Col. Orteese is again to take charge of us with a part of the same cavalry and escort us to Carettero [Querétaro].

Monday, 10th. Left San Louis for Carettaro, leaving 14 men behind in the hospital: [Levi] Williams, Boman [P. F. Bowman], Holderman, [Thomas] Tatum, J[ohn] Mills, [Charles] Hill, [John B.] Blanton, [David] Overton, [Peter] Rockyfellow, [William P.] Stapp, [Benjamin Z.] Boone, John Stansbury, J[ames] MacMicken & Winn [William Wynn].[106] From San Louis we were joined by about fifty pressed volunteers. Marched 5 leagues and camped for the night at a small town called Warloupa. San Louis is a pretty valley, though it is badly watered being supplied entirely by wells from which the most of the land in cultivation is watered. The valley, however, is badly cultivated and everything seems to be on the decline.

11th. Marched 21 miles to a small town called Elviguel Francisco.

12th. Marched 15 miles to a small town called Hasienda Akrol.

13th. Marched 27 miles to San Fillipe, south west course from San Louis.

14th. Marched 6 leagues and encamped at a poor ranch.

15th. Marched 18 miles to a small town Dolores, a pretty place with a fine church. At this place a memorable battle was fought between the Mexicans and Spaniards.[107]

16th. Marched 24 miles to San Maguel [Miguel]. This is a large town and situated on the side of a mountain, well watered by springs from the mountain. Through the politeness of our commander, Col. Orteese, about 20 of us were taken all through the town which is remarkable for its churches. Two of them we visited and were much pleased. They were extensive. One of them presented a very rich & gorgeous display of fine gilt work, with a large gallery of fine paintings attached to it. The other was more neatly finished and finely decorated and had the appearance of being lately finished though it would not have been executed by Mexicans as their genius for mechanism is at a rather low ebb.

We allso visited a place of resort for the fashionable ladies &

gentlemen of the city. It was a yard forming a half circle with seats on the side of the circle and surrounded by beautiful shade trees with a beautiful fountain of water in the middle or center. We found a number of fashionable ladies & gentlemen sitting round though there was no conversation between them as the ladies & gentlemen did not mix as is usual with the Mexicans or English & French on such occasions. A large number of the common class followed us, but did not presume to enter amongst the lords of fashion but kept a respectful distance and looked on at us untill we left, then they continued to follow us untill we reached our quarters. We were quite a ragged set and I felt rather bashful at being seen by ladies of fashion & taste.

17th. Marched 24 miles to Santa Rosa, a large hacienda.

18th. Marched 15 miles to Carettaro, a large town watered by a reservoy or conducter built at considerable expense, being built on pillars & arches 40 or 50 feet high across a valley several miles in length.

19th. Marched 12 miles to a hacienda called Seno.

20th. Marched 24 miles to a small town St. John Derio [San Juan del Río]. Here we overtook Adjt. Murray [Murry] who had been left sick by Fisher's party.

21st. Marched 42 miles and camped at a large hacienda, a stage stand. Here we conversed with an American who was on his way to Mexico and lived in Carettaro.

22nd. Marched 24 miles. Encamped up stairs in very dirty quarters.

23rd. Marched 4 leagues to Toula [Tula], a small town, and quartered in an old convent. Here we were joined by more volunteers. Together with those who had joined us at different places on the round, they numbered about 300. Here we were turned over to another officer from the city of Mexico who informed us that we had nothing to fear, that Packenham the English minister had requested him to treat us well and he intended to do so.

24th. Marched 8 leagues to the town of Uewatoka [Huehue-toca], were treated very bad on the road at night. We were locked up in close quartells which was remonstrated against but without effect.

At 8 o'clock Capt. Cameron was called out from us and told he was to be shot. [Alfred S.] Thurmond was allso taken out as interpreter but was not allowed to return.[108]

25th. Were joined by another old grey headed officer and some 10 or 12 more soldiers. We secured our days pay for rations, $7 to 4 men. This old officer was very kind and obliging to the men in changing their money, so much so that it attracted my attention. I saw him smile and pat several of the men on the check like a young lady would her lover and take their money and run off to get it changed. I now began to think he had been sent to execute some black deed and we soon learned that he had been sent to execute Cameron. His name I have not learned.

We marched 5 leagues and halted to rest. Were overtaken by the old officer and soon learned that our beloved & lamented Capt. Cameron had been shot. Thurmon was allowed to rejoin us. At 9 leagues we camped at a small town called Tampautla.

26th. Marched 9 miles to Mexico and confined in Santiago. We here found Dr. Sinicson, D[avid] Allen, Judge [Patrick] Usher, Mc [D. H.] Gattis, [John] Day [Morgan], Harvey Sellers, Gilbert Brush, J[ohn C. C.] Hill, and Jas. C. Wilson.[109] Crittenden left for his home.[110] These were men who had been left wounded & sick at Mier & Matamoras.

27th, 28th, 29th, 30th. Nothing important occurred. Visited by some foreigners and presented with a few clothes which are very acceptable.

1st, 2nd, 3rd, 4th, 5th. Nothing of importance. Through the foreign ministers have been furnished with a statement of the murder of the 17 men at the Salado and allso that of Cameron.

Saturday, 6th. All hands except a few sick at the hospital

chained two & two with heavy chains the size of a large log chain weighing from 12 to 15 lbs. and learn that we are to be put to work. We have already passed resolutions declaring we would not work for the tyrant Santa Anna, but the committee who drew up the resolution and signed it, strange to say, are with one exception all sick. We are advised by friends not to be stubborn in the matter. We reconsider the matter, appoint another committee to address the U. S. minister asking his advice.

This evening receive a large contribution of hats, shoes & clothing, principally from the French who are always friends to the Americans. Leathers have allso been brought in to make garatches [i.e., sandals]. Our commandant is much displeased because we would not receive them as we did not want anything from the government. He tells us that we shall have them and a full suit of striped lincey besides or a 1000 lashes.

Sunday, 7th. Our men make quite a respectable appearance being dressed in the clothes that their friends had given them, and we are again visited by a number of foreigners. Our bill of fare since we have been here is a cake of corn bread and a little corn flour gruel for breakfast, about 3 oz. of poor beef with soup and a cake of coarse bread for supper, beans half-cooked and a small cake of bread. These rations will keep soul and body together but never fatten.

Monday, 8th. Received a full suit of striped woolen cloth, hat & garatches in the bargain. Ordered to put them on immediately and prepare to march for Tackabayou [Tacubaya]. We soon appear in full uniform & are marched out under a guard of cavalry and armed with sand bags, wooden shovels, etc. We were marched some distance into the city and halted for a short time. Then we received some 25 or 30 heavy crobars and a large copper kettle to pack. We were now complete for service and marched out to Tackabayou, 2 leagues from city. About 1 o'clock we arrived in town and after marching & counter marching for some time, passing near the President's Palace, we were driven into a small room where we could not lay down. In an hour we were again taken out and marched about 1 league to an old church and again forced into another room too small to lay down.

9th. We were ordered to put on our uniforms to go and see the president, taking our tools etc. along. About 10 o'clock we arrived at the palace. All the rest were allowed to sit in the shade untill dinner and were then marched down to the foot of the street in a shady grove. Here the ladies presented us with cigars. We spent the evening here and returned to our quarters.

10th. Remained in prison. Nothing of importance occurred.

11th. Moved to quarters nearer the palace. Faired rather rough today. Compelled to pack all our provisions, cooking utensils, tools, bedding, etc. When we arrived at our quarters were much fatigued. Every man had a load as much as could cleverly wag with. Journey [Henry Journeay], a sick man, whipped for not carrying the load they gave him.[111]

12th. At work at the palace.

13th. At work this day I was struck by a criminal peon who was placed over us for an overseer. Without cause. I returned him the compliment over the head with a shovel and choked him in the bargain, for which I was afterwards severely beaten by a drunken soldier and the same overseer. I was allso compelled to carry three times as much sand as usual.

Sunday, 14th. In prison.

15th. I am unable to work. The men were at work as usual.

16th. The same as yesterday except the overseers have not whipped any of the men since Saturday.

17th. At work as usual.

18th. The same.

19th. Men at work all except the sick. The fair in rather rough and a good deal of possoming.

20th. As usual.

Sunday, 21st. In prison. Visited by Mr. Pratt & several others of the Americans and other foreigners who visit us on all convenient occasions.[112]

Monday, 22nd. J. [John] Shipman died at 3 o'clock in the morning. At 4 p.m. buried with a shroud and coffin.

23rd. As usual. All at work that are able. A good many puny and some not able to work.

24th. Nothing important. A dinner given us by the ladies of Tackabayou.

25th. 5 more of the Mier prisoners who were left wounded arrived. This is fast day and the men are not required to work. Seven of the sick left at San Louis & Carettaro have allso arrived some days ago, and John Blanton died the night after he arrived. [Bimoni] Middleton died on 6th.[113]

26th. Nothing important.

27th. Nothing of importance.

28th. Nothing of importance.

Monday, 29th. At work as usual.

Tuesday, 30th. About 1/2 of the men at work as usual packing sand. Santa Anna leaves Tackabayou on a visit of seven or eight days, some six or eight leagues distant. We allso learned that an account was published in the Mexican papers of an engagement between the Texian & Mexican fleets near Campeachy [Campeche] which lasted 11 hours, and the Texian fleet, it is stated, took refuge in the Bay of Campeachy.[114]

31st. About one third of the men are at work today packing sand and all the rest sick, or rather very much indisposed; 5 sent to the hospital rather against their wishes today. The best & largest rations of meat for dinner we have had in this city, although at best it is but poor and small.

June 1st, Thursday. About 2/3 of the men at work, the remainder indisposed. Some sent to the hospital.

Texians working on the road at Tacubaya.

McLaughlin, the artist, later settled in Brazoria County, where he died about 1852.

Friday, 2nd. The same as yesterday.

Saturday, 3rd. As yesterday pretty much. My companion P. M. Maxwell cut loose and sent to the hospital, [not] having worked a day in three weeks.[115] Only complaint rheumatism. This is a very good complaint to go to the hospital with as the patient is generally allowed enough to eat. In all other diseases starvation is resorted to. Although the patient may be debilitated in constitution and require nourishing food there is little chance of getting it. Consequently the men although unable to pack sand will stick to it a long time rather than go to the hospital.

Those who have been to the hospital inform us that the patients are stripped perfectly naked as they enter the establishment and are compelled to lay in bed the whole time they remain. Have cornmeal gruel to eat in small quantities and after undergoing a severe operation of salts & oil and several greasings, which is resorted to in almost all cases, the patient either dies or regains his appetite in which case he has to report himself well. He is then sent to a prison where there is a great many convicts called the casardo. After remaining here a few days he is sent to Santiago where he is fed as usual with beef soup etc. and in a few days sent out to this place to be put to work as soon as he is able.

This is an old establishment erected for the manufactory of powder some 80 or 100 years ago. The walls are falling down and all the timber decaying about the houses and no improvement going on to prevent it from falling down.

Sunday, 4th. Nothing important. No visitors to see us today.

5th. Nothing important. This is first day the men are ordered out to work and sent in again at noon.

Tuesday, 6th. Feast day but the men are all at work notwithstanding except those that are indisposed. I am again cut loose from John McMullin my old companion, and chained to Mr. Vandyke [Wilson M. Van Dyke] who is rather unwell.[116]

Wednesday, 8th. At work as yesterday. Santa Anna returns to Tackabayou. We are allso visited by several foreigners who inform us that the Mexican government are withdrawing all their forces destined to act against Yucatan to put down about 3000 Indians who were in arms against the government in south Mexico. We allso learn further particulars of the Mexican account of the naval action with Com. Moore. They report both of their war steamers much injured and allso Com. Moore's flag ship which they say ran into the shallow water as they could not follow there and after the engagement the steam ship Warloupe ran into the bay of Campeachy to get water and the most of her crew captured by the Yucatans while getting water. It is allso anticipated that the difficulty between Texas and Mexico will be settled between this and fall. It is probable that this opinion exists under the supposition that Texas will accede to the propositions made by Santa Anna. This however is a delusive hope as Texas cannot with honour to herself stop short of anything but total independence which she has both the ability & force to maintain against any such government as Mexico. We allso learn that the new constitution for the government of the Mexican Republic will be presented to Santa Anna for his approval next week and it is said that it is draughted by creatures of his own choice. Under these circumstances it is reasonable to suppose he will approve of it and it is anticipated a revolution or civil war will follow.

Thursday, 8th. Nothing very important since we have been here. We have had many reports about being released on the 13th of June, the present month. All are in great hopes it may be true, but fear to believe it too confidently as the Mexicans so seldom tell the truth that our general rule is always to anticipate just the reverse of what they say. In this case however we have waived the general rule and the most of the men have a good deal of confidence in the reports.

Friday, 9th. Today I volunteer to work in hopes of improving health though my partner Vandyke is taken with a fever and we lay in the shade in the afternoon; 22 of the men return from the hospital.

Saturday, 10th. 14 men sent to the hospital and all the rest who came yesterday chained. I am again cut loose & chained to my old messmate, P. H. Lusk. The men at work today say they had a great many officers overseeing them today, and they worked harder than usual, and nearly completed the job which is a piece of road about

150 feet long and 30 wide. Any six of us with a horse & cart with our own management could have done the same labour in 10 days whereas it has employed from 75 to 120 men 26 days & ½ under the superintendence of both civil & military officers. One of the colonels treated the men to a loaf of bread and a glass of liquer.

Sunday, 11th. In prison. Nothing important.

Monday, 12th. The men are at work repairing the road in the worst places. Hopes of liberty are getting faint.

Tuesday, 13th. This is Santa Anna's birthday. He issued an order to release all political prisoners but we have not yet ascertained whether we are included or not.

Wednesday, 14th. The men are taken to work on the road again and we are visited by our old friend the Frenchman who is confident Santa Anna's order does not include us, and nearly all of us are without any hope of liberty untill the existing difficulties between Texas & Mexico are settled.

Thursday, 15th. This is the national feast day of Mexico and we are not at work.

Friday, 16th. At work on the road between Tackabayou and the city of Mexico filling up the mud holes etc.

Saturday, 17th. J[ohn] Owens died after a very short illness of about 48 hours.[117] At work as yesterday. Santa Anna is expected to return from the city. We are paraded and wait some time after 5 o'clock for him to pass without seeing him. We then marched to our quarters. We allso heard again we were to be liberated very shortly.

Sunday, 18th. In prison. We receive letters from Perote. We are told by the commandant that the reason we had not been released was because the Texians have been doing a great deal of mischief about Santa Fe. I hope this may be true.[118]

Monday, 19th. Robert Smith died; 22 men came from the hospital. At work again at the old place near the president's palace breaking up the work which we have done several times over already and a part of us packing rock & stone from the bayou a half mile distant.

Tuesday, 21st. At work as yesterday. Heavy rain $\frac{1}{2}$ past 4 o'clock; all hands very wet. Receive information again that we will be liberated shortly.

Wednesday, 21st. Misty and light rains in the morning. Go to work at 10 o'clock. Major Murray came from the hospital, [William] Morris allso.[119]

Thursday, 22nd. We have a new guard. At work as usual.

Friday, 23rd. Another new guard. At work as yesterday. Nothing else to report out.

Saturday, 24th. At work as usual. Nothing of importance. The guard continues to be changed daily.

Sunday, 25th. In prison. Today visited by two foreigners who furnish us with some papers, Spanish & American. We see that Santa Anna has again declared that no prisoners shall be taken in the war with Texas in consequence of the late expedition against Santa Fe & Moore in the gulph.

Dr. McMath addressed a letter to Santa Anna on the subject of our rations.

Monday, 26th. At work as usual. Nothing important.

Friday, 27th. Nothing important in the way of news. [Thomas] Colville died of damp cholic with the chains on him.

Wednesday, 28th. Colville was buried at the expense of the B. [British] Consul. Reports say that Yucatan has come to terms and Com. Moore is likely allso to be taken.

Thursday, 29th. This is feast day. No work.

Friday, 30th. At work. Nothing important.

Saturday, 1st July. Nothing important.

Sunday, 2nd. Visited by a number of foreigners who gave us twelve dollars.

Monday, 3rd. At work as usual. Address a letter to Santa Anna requesting the privilege of celebrating the anniversary of the Independence of the U. S., which privilege is granted.

July 4th. We remained in our prison and celebrated the anniversary of the independence of the U. S. of America. Resolutions & toasts were regularly drawn up suitable to the occasion. The Star Spangled Banner was sung and a spirited address was delivered by Judge [Fenton M.] Gibson. The Mexican officers of the guard were invited to attend and some of them became highly insulted by Judge Gibson's remarks and gestures which they partly understood. The Americans in the city have a grand celebration commencing late in the evening and two of them try to get permission for some of our officers to join them but without success.[120]

Wednesday, 5th. Visited by W. [Waddy] Thompson, U. S. minister. He informs us that Sam Houston has published his proclamation recalling all the Texian forces for a cessation of arms. At work as usual.

Thursday, 6th. Nothing important.

Friday, 7th. Nothing important. At work as usual. The British minister sends us word that we may expect to be released in the present month. Our commander is allso changed and some hopes of better living in the future; 21 men return from the hospital. The men, generally speaking, are in high spirits.

Saturday, 8th. Nothing important more than the confirmation of yesterday's report that Santa Anna had agreed to the armistice and great hopes are entertained of our release in a short time. John Hill, a boy of sixteen, is set at liberty by Santa Anna.[121]

Sunday, 9th. Some changes in our rations. Great parade & new arrangements made for conducting the work on the street of Tacubaya. All the interpreters and officers are unchained and appointed to different squads; are held responsible for the labour of the others, and if they do not do their duty and make the men work, they are to be put to work themselves. Today we are visited by several foreigners. No other important information.

Monday, 10th. Instead of packing sand our selves·we have burros furnished us. The criminal overseers are not allowed to whip the men and we do a great deal more work than usual.

Tuesday, 11th. Everything goes on pretty smoothly. The men are in better health from a change of diet but are still dissatisfied as the quantity is insufficient to satisfy the cravings of hunger.

Wednesday, 12th. Everything went on pretty much as yesterday. We are informed that Santa Anna says he will release us as soon as we finish a certain piece of road which is now about 300 yards long. We have little confidence in this assurance or we would finish it in a very short time.

Thursday, 13th. At work as yesterday. Nothing else important.

Friday, 14th. We learn by report that 4 of the 16 prisoners that made their escape from Perote castle was retaken and shot on the coast.

Saturday, 15th. Everything went on pretty much as yesterday. We learn that the Texians have actually arrived in Santa Fe and sixteen hundred government troops have been sent to meet them. Nothing else important.

Sunday, 16th. For the first time I am permitted to have my irons taken off in consequence of the interposition of Judge Gibson who assured the Colonel that I was a good hand to work. The report of the four prisoners who were lately retaken being shot is contradicted. Judge Gibson, [William] Ryon & William Moore have leave to go to the city today. They conversed with W. [Waddy] Thompson and learned that the rumour was actually cited that Sam Houston had denounced us.[122]

Monday, 17th. At work as usual. Nothing of importance.

Tuesday, 18th. As yesterday at work.

Wednesday, 19th. James S. White is put in double irons because he will not go out to work in consequence of his being severely afflicted with the rheumatic pains.[123] He is allso put in close & solitary confinement in a damp and filthy room.

Thursday, 20th. At work as usual. Nothing else important.

Friday, 21st. Pretty much as yesterday.

Saturday, 22nd. Nothing important.

Sunday, 23rd. In prison. A number of the men are unchained and we learn that all of them are to be unchained between now and next Wednesday. Wm. Beard died this morning at 6 o'clock. His brother died at San Louis Potosi. They were both brave soldiers, unassuming in their manners and much beloved by their comrades.

Monday, 4th. At work. Nothing of particular importance.

Tuesday, 25th. Nothing important.

Wednesday, 26th. At work. Nothing important.

Thursday, 27th. Carter Sargeant died at the hospital. Nothing else important.

Friday, 28th. At work on the street. As yesterday nothing else important.

Saturday, 29th. At work as usual.

Sunday, 30th. Nothing very important, except W. [Willis] Copeland's having made his escape from prison last night is not yet discovered by the Mexicans.[124] And having contemplated doing the same thing myself as soon as I received money sufficient, myself and friend Jas. C. Willson and Mc Gattis came to the conclusion that if we deferred it any longer until they discovered Copeland had made his escape, which they would certainly do the next morning, our chance for the future would be very small as we all expected to be rechained on Monday morning and not allowed to step out of doors after sun set. With these considerations we determined on trying to make our escape. Willson and myself on this evening had the pleasure of a walk in the park of the military academy which is about two leagues from the city and is closely connected with our prison yard. One of the greatest curiosities we saw was the secret passage which it is said Montazuma had to the city. However, the most interesting part of our walk to me was to examine the walls for the purpose of getting out. We passed the sentinels at the doors early in the night and scaled the walls about 8 o'clock splitting our blankets and tieing them together for the purpose of letting ourselves down with.[125]

We passed through the city. About eleven o'clock we climbed over the two gates on the Warloupe road and walked very brisk. When we arrived at the village of Warloupe we found a soldier on post at the gate. We turned to the right side. Proceeded on the ditch about one mile or less but finding no crossing place we were compelled to swim it. At daybreak we left the road.

On the morning of the 31st July we stowed ourselves away under a bunch of bushes to spend the day in secret repose, but we were much disappointed as we happened to be in a place where all the shepherd boys of the town came along and we were near being discovered several times. At length we determined to move our position so we started across the mountain when nearly sunset we were discovered by two Mexicans who were gathering aughmeal [*aguamiel*] from the megay [i.e., *maguey*]. They inquired our business etc. and then told us to go with them to the town and shew our passports. This we objected to but they insisted and we could only get clear of them by giving them one dollar which was all we had and promised them 25 more. They agreed not to say anything about us, but we thought it best to lay close until night. We then recommenced our march, and crossed the mountain close by, fearing the road in the pass might be guarded. We marched about six leagues and halted at day break near a small town.

August 1st. We lay close all day in the best hiding place we could find, but we were a little surprised about sunset when four Mexicans with sharp sticks [i.e., bayonets], as the Texians call them, came and marched us off to see the Alcalde. He asked us for our passports which we could not produce. He told us he would send us back to Mexico to see the Prefect. We told him we had no money. Upon close examination, however, we found we had one picayune left which we all suped on.

We were then taken up town and shut up in an old gaol which was allso used as a school house. They locked us up and contrary to our expectations they left no sentinel at the door. We laid down about one hour until everything got still. We then to be assured there was no one about, rapped several times at the door and called for water. No persons answered. I then began to try and pick the lock with a pair of old scissors but couldn't succeed. I then began to examine the hinge of the door which was of the older stile though very substantial. I thought though by the aid of the leavers we had which were used for bushes I could succeed in making an opening large enough to get out of it and I continued operations and in one hour we succeeded in getting out.

We marched rapidly untill daybreak Wednesday morning and hid ourselves on the top of a hill close to a small town and remained till night not undiscovered however as the shepherd boys were all around us, and one of them discovered us. But we soon moved our position where we remained untill night and took the road and after traveling some three or four leagues we found out we were on the elongated valley. We climbed the mountains and at day break Thursday we halted and hid in the bushes on the side of a mountain and remained till night. We then took the trail which led us to a small hut where we inquired the road.

In about an hour after this we met two Mexicans who appeared to be much alarmed, crying out to know what nation we were but would not come near enough to receive an answer. We continued our march on the road. In about $\frac{3}{4}$ of an hour they returned and demanded us to halt but would not come nearer than long rifle shot distance. They wanted us to go back to the town. This we objected to telling them we had our passports which we supposed would be good; that we worked in the mines at Mineral Del Monte, that we were already two days behind our time and as for going back we could not think of it. Willson pulled an old song ballad of "When Shall We Three Meet Again" and endeavoured to get them to look at it but could not get near enough to show it to them. They agreed however to go with us to the next ranch where they could get a light and examine it. He told them it made no material difference about the light as he could interpret it to them by moon light as it was written in English.

They proceeded on, however, untill we came to a ranch. We all stepped in with the boldness and self importance of Englishmen and our companion J. C. Willson took out his song ballad again and told them it was a passport written in English for all three of us. They told him to translate it. He told them that he could not translate very well, but he would satisfy them that the passports were genuine. He commenced and translated a pretty good passport out of the song ballad. They said it was bueno and then apologized for detaining us stating that they thought we were bad men. We told them that we did not blame them atall, that their regulations were essentially necessary and they had only done their duty. We proceeded on laughing very hearty at the hoax we had played off on them.

At daybreak Friday, 5th, we were close to Mineral Del Monte but could not get in before day light as our friend J. C. Willson had become so weak from debility of constitution and starvation since we left that he could not walk half a mile without lying down to rest. So we stayed up on the mountain to lay by during the day. We saw several shepherds in the course of the day and they all wanted to know what we were doing there. We told them that we were minerologists and were hunting small specimens of ore etc. for the English mining company. That appeared perfectly satisfactory. In the course of the day we satisfied ourselves of the position of the town and succeeded in getting in about 8 o'clock at night. Here we found friends who done considerable for us.

Saturday, 5th. Remained at Mineral del Monte untill 7 o'clock at night and took up the line of march for Tampico, leaving our friend Willson behind too unwell to travel.[126] We marched through a town called Grandee, laid down near the road, and slept till daylight Sunday, 6th, and resumed our march. Passed through Zaquatapan [Zacualtipán], 13 leagues. Slept by the roadside until Monday morning, 7th. We are in a hilly though a very beautiful country covered with timber of various description, the little valleys all thickly settled and hillsides so steep that a man might break his neck by a misstep. Covered with fine crops of corn. We marched 13 leagues and slept near Potipcan. Awakened near day, Tuesday, 8th, by a heavy rain and resumed our march through mud and mire. Marched about 12 leagues and camped in an Indian village 3 leagues from Pesca.

Wednesday, 9th. Marched 13 leagues to a small town called Tontiuca [Tantoyuca] and slept for the night here. We were required to show our passports which were pronounced good.

Thursday, 10th. Marched 18 leagues to Oslewauma [Ozuluama] and slept near the roadside.

Friday, 11th. Marched 12 leagues and slept at a house.

Saturday, 12th. Marched 6 leagues to Tampico, Old Town, and from thence to Tampico by water in a canoe, and after walking around for some time we found the U. S. consul and took lodgings at the house of a Frenchman.

Sunday, 13th. Remained at the house of the Frenchman in doors. At night we were visited by Mr. C., U. S., and afterwards introduced to Mr. W. and went to his house and took lodgings where we remained untill 4 o'clock Monday, 14th, and started up the river with Mr. L. to await the departure of a vessel.[127] Here we remained untill September 2nd, working some to pay our board and pass off the time more agreeably.

September 3rd. I embarked on board the schooner Richard St. John, Capt. Everson, master. My friend Gattis embarked on board of the schooner Brassos bound for New York. I soon found another comrade on the Richard St. John, John Dalrymple, one of the Perote prisoners who had made his escape about the last of June. He had shipped as cook and I shipped as seaman.[128] Our vessel being a good sailer and easily managed, we arrived at the Balise and crossed the bar on the 9th against head winds nearly all the way. At a little past sunset we were taken in tow by the Texian steamer Sarah Barnes from Galveston.[129]

NOTES

1. Edmund L. Dana, *Incidents in the Life of Capt. Samuel H. Walker, Texan Ranger*, p. 49. Dana served with Walker in Mexico and later wrote a number of letters to old acquaintances collecting additional information. Their responses are in his papers deposited with the Wyoming Historical and Geological Society.

2. James M. Day, *Black Beans & Goose Quills*, lists and discusses the various known accounts of the expedition.

3. Albert G. Brackett, *General Lane's Brigade in Central Mexico*, p. 77; J. H. Kuykendall, "Sketches of Early Texians," University Archives, Barker Texas History Center, University of Texas at Austin, p. 8; James Charles Wilson, *Address on the Occasion of Removing the Remains of Captains Walker and Gillespie on the 21st of April, A.D., 1856*, p. 14.

4. J. Jacob Oswandel, *Notes of the Mexican War, 1846–47–48*, p. 24; Kuykendall, "Sketches," p. 8; Brackett, *Lane's Brigade*, p. 92.

5. Oswandel, *Notes*, p. 354.

6. Samuel C. Reid, *The Scouting Expeditions of McCulloch's Texas Rangers*, p. 188; *Graham's American Monthly Magazine* (June 1848), 301; Dana, *Incidents*, p. 44; James M. Day, "Samuel H. Walker," in *Rangers of Texas*, by James M. Day et al., pp. 31–32; "Samuel H. Walker" in Public Debt Papers, Archives Division, Texas State Library, Austin. Reid gives Walker's birthdate as 1817, as does *The Handbook of Texas*, 3:1076. Walter Prescott Webb, *The Texas Rangers: A Century of Frontier Defense*, p. 84, gives it as 1810. Walker's tombstone indicates 1815.

7. "Sketch of Colonel John C. Hays, Texas Ranger," from materials furnished by Colonel Hays and Major John Caperton, University Archives, Barker Texas History Center, University of Texas at Austin.

8. The definitive work on the events of 1842 recounted in Walker's journal is Joseph Milton Nance, *Attack and Counterattack: The Texas-Mexican Frontier, 1842*.

9. For a discussion of the influence of Green's book on other literature on the subject, see Day, *Black Beans*, pp. 134, 137, 145.

10. Eugene C. Barker and Amelia W. Williams, eds., *The Writings of Sam Houston*, 3:300.

11. John C. Duval, *The Adventures of Big-Foot Wallace*, p. 167.

12. The journal is in the Southern Historical Collection, University of North

Carolina at Chapel Hill, under the group title Diary of Sam H. Walker #3652. I am indebted to Richard A. Shrader for permission to publish the journal.

While in prison Walker wrote a letter to Albert Sidney Johnston, partially summarizing the content of the diary (see Walker to Johnston, May 4, 1843, Army Papers, Republic of Texas, Archives Division, Texas State Library, Austin).

13. See Oswandel, *Notes*, pp. 176, 182; Webb, *Texas Rangers*, p. 116.

14. Oswandel, *Notes*, pp. 117, 198.

15. Walker to Houston [copy], October 28, 1843, Thomas Jefferson Green Papers, Southern Historical Collection, University of North Carolina at Chapel Hill.

16. S. H. Walker to T. J. Green, November 9, 1843, ibid.

17. Kuykendall, "Sketches," p. 8.

18. T. J. Green to S. H. Walker, November 8, 1843, Green Papers.

19. Barker and Williams, *Writings*, 4:437–441.

20. See Day, *Black Beans*, pp. 54–66; Sam Houston, *Speech . . . on Texan Affairs . . . Thomas Jefferson Green*; and Thomas J. Green, *Reply of . . . to the Speech of Gen. Sam Houston in the Senate of the United States, August 4, 1854*.

21. John E. Parsons, ed., *Sam Colt's Own Record*, p. 105.

22. Ibid., p. 9.

23. Walter Prescott Webb, *The Great Plains*, pp. 178–179.

24. Parsons, *Colt's Own Record*, p. 10.

25. See Mary A. Maverick, *Memoirs*, pp. 81–83; Reid, *Scouting Expeditions*, pp. 109–111; Dana, *Incidents*, pp. 47–49. Maverick gives the date as June 8, 1844. Dana's account is the best and is told in the words of W. S. Oury, a participant.

26. Parsons, *Colt's Own Record*, p. 81.

27. Dana, *Incidents*, p. 49.

28. House Executive Documents 60, 30 Cong., 1 Sess., pp. 289–290, 292–294, Serial 520; Dana, *Incidents*, pp. 50–54.

29. House Executive Documents 4, 29 Cong., 2 Sess., pp. 102–108, Serial 497.

30. Walter P. Lane, *Adventures and Recollections of . . .*, p. 47.

31. Parsons, *Colt's Own Record*, pp. 8–9.

32. Ibid.

33. Ibid., p. 10.

34. Ibid.

35. Ibid., pp. 112–113.

36. Ibid., pp. 60, 64–65, 74–76.

37. Charles T. Haven, *The History of the Colt Revolver*, p. 293.

38. Oswandel, *Notes*, p. 350.

39. For an appraisal of *The Brave Ranger*, see Lota M. Spell, *Pioneer Printer: Samuel Bangs in Mexico and Texas*, p. 132.

40. Wilson, *Address*.

41. The three Walker Colt revolvers identified as having belonged to Sam Walker are featured in R. L. Wilson, *Samuel Colt Presents: A Loan Exhibition of Presentation Percussion Colt Firearms*, pp. 28–30. See also, R. L. Wilson, *The Arms Collection of Samuel Colt*, p. 16. Mr. Wilson is the acknowledged authority on Colt firearms and has written widely on the subject. As the pistols were issued in pairs, it is his belief that Walker had two pairs, one pair presented to him by Sam Colt and the other pair issued by the army. The fate of the fourth pistol is unknown. (R. L. Wilson to editor, November 14, 1977.) I am indebted to Mr. Wilson for guidance in search of Walker material and for his interest in this work.

For the history of the sword, see Dana, *Incidents*, pp. 1–40.

42. For details of the Vásquez raid, see Nance, *Attack and Counterattack*, pp. 9–54.

43. Walker refers to Houston's statement, dated March 21, 1842, which appears in Barker and Williams, *Writings*, 2:513–537.

Alexander Somervell was born in Maryland in 1796 and came to Texas in 1833. He fought in the Battle of San Jacinto and served in the Texas Congress, 1836–1838. Houston appointed him a customs collector after the failure of the 1842 expedition. Somervell died under mysterious circumstances in 1854. (Ibid., p. 493; Sam Houston Dixon and Louis Wiltz Kemp, *The Heroes of San Jacinto*, pp. 157–158.)

44. The engagement is described in Nance, *Attack and Counterattack*, pp. 229–254.

Ewen Cameron emerged as the hero-martyr of the Mier Expedition. Walker later recounts the circumstances of his death. Born in Scotland about 1811, Cameron came to Texas during the Texas Revolution and in the period that followed won renown as the leader of the "cowboys" in south Texas. Active in frontier defense, he was hailed as "a bold and chivalrous leader" who promised to become "the Bruce of the West" by the Houston *Telegraph and Texas Register*, September 14, 1842. (*Handbook of Texas*, 1:275.)

James Davis was born in Virginia on July 17, 1790, and fought in the Battle of New Orleans with Andrew Jackson. He came to Texas in 1834, developed a plantation in Liberty County, and represented that county in the Texas Congress of 1843–1844 and at the Annexation Convention in 1845. He died February 10, 1859. (*Handbook of Texas*, 3:230.)

45. For the Mexican account of the engagement, see Joseph Milton Nance, trans. and ed., "Brigadier General Adrian Woll's Report of His Expedition into Texas in 1842," *Southwestern Historical Quarterly* 58 (April 1955), 523–552.

46. Mathew Caldwell, familiarly known as Old Paint, was fresh from his imprisonment in Mexico as a result of his participation in the Santa Fe Expedition. His sufferings impaired his health and he died December 28, 1842, only a few months after the Woll campaign. No doubt, his health affected his leadership, for previously he had won renown for his daring. Born in 1788, he came to Texas in 1831. He fought in the opening battle of the Texas Revolution at Gonzales, signed the Texas Declaration of Independence, and later

fought in the Council House Fight and Battle of Plum Creek. (George R. Nielsen, "Mathew Caldwell," *Southwestern Historical Quarterly* 64 [April 1961], 478–502.)

47. For a biography of John Coffee Hays, see James K. Greer, *Colonel Jack Hays: Texas Frontier Leader and California Builder.*

48. Jesse Billingsley, born in Tennessee on October 10, 1810, came to Texas in 1834 and settled near Bastrop. He commanded a company of volunteers in the Battle of San Jacinto and received a wound that crippled his left hand for life. A noted captain of the Texas Rangers, he served in the Congress of the Republic of Texas and later in the Texas state legislature. He died October 1, 1880. (Dixon and Kemp, *Heroes of San Jacinto*, pp. 157–158.)

49. Walker characteristically avoids identifying a companion when his observation is critical. Nance, *Attack and Counterattack*, p. 368, identifies the other scout as Cicero Rufus Perry.

50. For other accounts of the Dawson battlefield by contemporaries, see Z. N. Morrill, *Flowers and Fruits in the Wilderness*, pp. 170–172; Catherine W. McDowell, ed., *Now You Hear My Horn: The Journal of James Wilson Nichols*, pp. 103–105.

51. James S. Mayfield was born in Tennessee in 1809 and emigrated to Texas in 1837. He represented Nacogdoches in the Texas Congress, 1840–1842, and served briefly as Secretary of State in 1841. Later he moved to Fayette County. (Elizabeth LeNoir Jennett, *Biographical Directory of the Texan Conventions and Congresses, 1832–1845*, pp. 135–136.)

52. Samuel H. Luckie recovered from his wound and lived until October 30, 1852. He came to Texas from Georgia before 1837 and represented Bexar County in the Congress of the Republic of Texas, 1841–1842. He was one of Jack Hay's "Minute Men" in 1841. (Ibid., p. 127; Morrill, *Flowers and Fruits*, p. 175.)

53. John Henry Moore was born in Tennessee in 1800 and moved to Texas in 1821. The original owner of the town site of La Grange, he developed a large plantation in Fayette County. Moore gained renown as an Indian fighter and was an early advocate of Texan independence. He died in 1880. (Barker and Williams, *Writings*, 2:426.)

54. At this time, Edward Burleson was vice-president of the Republic of Texas. An old acquaintance described him as a "good, clever, good-humored jovial fellow" but expressed surprise at his election to high civil office. "I knew 'Ned Burleson' 20 odd years ago, and then no one could even have dreamed of predicting that he would ever have been 'thought of' as the vice president of a republic nation," wrote Josiah Gregg. Born in North Carolina in 1798, Burleson migrated to Texas in 1831 and settled near Bastrop, where he won renown as an Indian fighter. In the fall of 1835, he succeeded Stephen F. Austin in command of the army before Bexar, and in the Battle of San Jacinto he served as colonel of the first regiment of Texas Volunteers. He was elected to the Texas Congress in 1834 and to the vice-presidency in 1841. He died December 23, 1851, in Austin. (Josiah Gregg, *Diary and Letters of . . .:*

Southwestern Enterprises, 1840–1847, 1:110; Dixon and Kemp, *Heroes of San Jacinto,* pp. 125–216.)

55. Joseph L. Bennett came to Texas in 1834 and served as a lieutenant colonel in the Battle of San Jacinto. In 1837 Sam Houston appointed him colonel of a frontier defense regiment. The following year he was elected to the Texas Congress from Montgomery County. He died in Freestone County in 1848. The militia he commanded in 1842 generally received a bad press. (Dixon and Kemp, *Heroes of San Jacinto,* pp. 292–293; McDowell, *Now You Hear My Horn,* pp. 89–90.)

56. Other contemporary accounts of the march include James M. Day, ed., "Israel Canfield on the Mier Expedition," *Texas Military History* 3 (Fall 1963), 165–199; idem., "Diary of James A. Glasscock, Mier Man," *Texana* 1 (Spring–Summer 1963), 85–119, 225–238; Thomas W. Bell, *A Narrative of the Capture and Subsequent Sufferings of the Mier Prisoners in Mexico,* James M. Day, ed.; William P. Stapp, *The Prisoners of Perote,* pp. 23–24 (pagination of 1845 ed.).

57. William Alsbury fell asleep with his head on his prisoner's body, whereupon the prisoner gently removed the head to a saddle and departed (Sterling Brown Hendricks, "The Somervell Expedition to the Rio Grande, 1842," *Southwestern Historical Quarterly* 23 [October 1919], 123; John Henry Brown, *History of Texas from 1685 to 1892,* 2:237).

58. See Nance, *Attack and Counterattack,* p. 507. James R. Cook came to Texas in 1831 and settled first at Liberty and then at Columbus, where he engaged in business. He fought in the Battle of San Jacinto. Cook was killed in a drunken row at Washington on the Brazos on March 31, 1843, shortly after he returned from the Somervell Expedition. (Dixon and Kemp, *Heroes of San Jacinto,* p. 311.)

59. Although several accounts mention the death of Dubois or De Boyce, none identifies him more fully (see Duval, *Big-Foot Wallace,* p. 168; Stapp, *Prisoners,* p. 24; Hendricks, "Somervell Expedition," p. 127).

60. The plunder of Laredo was widely condemned (see Bell, *Narrative,* pp. 9–10; Houston *Morning Star,* January 17, 1843; Nance, *Attack and Counterattack,* pp. 521–526).

61. William S. Fisher was born in Virginia and came to Texas in 1834. He settled in Gonzales, which he represented in the consultation in 1835. He served as captain of the first regiment of Texas Volunteers, Co. I, in the Battle of San Jacinto, and was elected a member of the First Congress of the Republic of Texas. Fisher was appointed Secretary of War by Sam Houston, and lieutenant colonel of a frontier regiment by Mirabeau B. Lamar. Wounded at Mier, Fisher was generally criticized by the men he led in the battle. He survived imprisonment at Perote and was released September 16, 1844, by the Mexican government, but did not survive long thereafter. He died in Jackson County in 1845 but lived long enough to read and criticize Green's book on the Mier Expedition. (Dixon and Kemp, *Heroes of San Jacinto,* p. 253.)

62. Ben McCulloch, born in 1811 in Tennessee, arrived in Texas in time to

command one of the "Twin Sisters" in the Battle of San Jacinto. After adventures on the frontier with the Texas Rangers, he moved to California in 1849. He returned to Texas in 1852. McCulloch died in the Battle of Elk Horn, March 7, 1862, as a Confederate general. (Jack W. Gunn, "Ben McCulloch, Big Captain," *Southwestern Historical Quarterly* 58 [July 1954], 1–21.)

63. Young Jesse Yokum, whose name is variously spelled, came from a Liberty County family that was sometimes of doubtful reputation. In his "Diary," p. 88 (Day, ed.,) Glasscock wrote that Yokum was "accidentally killed by a Mr. Hill." See also, Day, "Mier Expedition," p. 169; and "Jesse Yokum," in Houston Wade Papers, Archives Division, Texas State Library, Austin.

Gideon K. Lewis, familiarly known as "Legs" and reputedly a devil with the ladies, survived many adventures to be killed by an irate husband in 1855. Born in Ohio about 1823, he edited a newspaper in Galveston after the Mier Expedition and with Samuel Bangs founded the Matamoros *Reveille* in 1846. Later Lewis formed a partnership with Richard King and accumulated a large estate, primarily in land. As he left neither will nor heirs, the settlement of his estate was a lengthy process. (Tom Lea, *The King Ranch*, 1:99–110, 131–136; Spell, *Samuel Bangs*, pp. 129–130.)

Allen Holderman, a native of Kentucky, resided at Bastrop. He did not survive the expedition. (Thomas J. Green, *Journal of the Texian Expedition against Mier*, pp. 439, 444; Day, "Mier Expedition," p. 69; Day, "Diary," p. 88.)

64. I.e., *escopetas*, which Big-Foot Wallace described as "short, bell-mouthed, bull-doggish looking" muskets, carrying a very heavy ball and shooting with little accuracy (Duval, *Big-Foot Wallace*, p. 173).

65. Again Walker is somewhat critical of his companions and refrains from identifying them. The other scout captured with him was Patrick H. Lusk, son of Samuel Lusk of Washington on the Brazos. An uncle was a special friend of Andrew Jackson, who used his influence to obtain Patrick Lusk's release. (Green, *Journal*, pp. 440, 445; Day, "Mier Expedition," p. 169; Day, "Diary," p. 88; Jonnie Lockhart Wallis and Laurance L. Hill, comps., *Sixty Years on the Brazos*, pp. 44, 186.)

Canfield and Glasscock give somewhat different versions of Walker's capture, writing that he was "decoyed" away from his company. See also, A. J. Sowell, *The Life of Big-Foot Wallace*, p. 19; Day, "S. H. Walker," p. 35.

66. D. H. E. Beasley, a native of North Carolina and resident of Brazoria, was released by the Mexican government September 16, 1844 (Green, *Journal*, pp. 437, 476).

Richard Keene and his brother Edward, originally from Kentucky, lived at Washington, Texas. Richard Keene was among those who, like Charles K. Reese, refused to participate in the escape at Salado. The brothers escaped from Perote on March 25, 1844. (Green, *Journal*, pp. 437, 440, 450, 476; Houston Wade, *Notes and Fragments*, 2:111–118.)

Dr. John J. Sinnickson, a native of New Jersey, resided at Brazoria. His role at Mier was much criticized, and when he was released from prison through the intercession of Waddy Thompson, Stapp (*Prisoners*, pp. 101–102) wrote, "To our mutual gratification, we got rid of Dr. ――― here, being the worthy who brought us the white flag at Mier, and who was ever after execrated by the men for urging our surrender . . . Conscious of the odium in which he was held, he sought to resent it by a base neglect of such of the soldiers as were dependent upon his aid; suffering them to die in the same room with himself, for the want of those services they were too destitute to command."

Sinnickson's explanation of his conduct appears in Green, *Journal*, pp. 474–476.

67. Other firsthand accounts of the battle appear in Stapp, *Prisoners*, pp. 37–39; Day, "Mier Expedition," pp. 169–171; Bell, *Narrative*, pp. 13–18; Day, "Diary," pp. 89–90. Official records, including "Names of 263 Men Composing Col. William S. Fisher's Command Capitulated at Mier, December 26, 1942," are in Army Papers, Mier Expedition, Republic of Texas, Archives Division, Texas State Library, Austin.

Joseph Berry was born in Indiana before 1813 and came to Texas with his father, a gunsmith, in 1826. The large family settled at Bastrop. Berry was killed by a Mexican as he lay immobilized by his broken leg, a circumstance that outraged his companions. (Wade, *Notes and Fragments*, 1:24–25; John J. Linn, *Reminiscences of Fifty Years in Texas*, p. 318.)

Whitfield Chalk was born in North Carolina on April 4, 1811, and came to Texas about 1839. He fought Indians under Edward Burleson's command and joined in the defense of San Antonio after Woll's raid. His companion in the escape described here is identified variously as Caleb or William St. Clair, a native of New York and resident of Gonzales. A slightly different version of their escape appears in Olive Todd Walker, "Major Whitfield Chalk, Hero of the Republic of Texas," *Southwestern Historical Quarterly* 60 (January 1957), 359–368. Chalk died May 18, 1902, aged 92, in Lampasas County.

Vásquez, first name unknown, was described by Joseph D. McCutchan, another participant, as "a Mexican who had been with the Texians and accompanied them to the banks of the Alcantro, from whence he suddenly disappeared." McCutchan also told of the Mexican soldiers' search among the captives for "one Mexican named Bascus, who had formerly been a rober [*sic*] among them. Bascus . . . had been with us and had even made his appearance among us after crossing, but was not taken with us." (Joseph D. McCutchan, "Narrative of the Mier Expedition," Archives, Rosenberg Library, Galveston, Texas, pp. 63, 89.) This was probably the same man described by John Henry Brown, *Indian Wars and Pioneers of Texas*, p. 66, as "old Vasquez, a New Madrid Spaniard in our company at the battle of Salado."

68. Samuel McDade died of his wounds on January 4, 1843, at New Reinosa (Wade, *Notes and Fragments*, 1:128; Bell, *Narrative*, p. 82; Day, "Mier Expedition," p. 172).

69. The kindness of James D. Marks, United States consul, and Joseph P. Schatzell, a German merchant who formerly lived in Kentucky, was noted by

a number of the captives. Schatzell gave $5 to each Kentuckian and "there was more than the usual number of Kentuc Boys about this time," wrote Canfield in "Mier Expedition" (Day, ed.), pp. 172–173. "Mr. S. also advanced several hundred dollars on drafts drawn by several of our party some of which are I think worthless." See also, Day, "Diary," p. 92, and letter of J. D. Cocke in Houston *Morning Star*, March 4, 7, 1843.

70. From this point Green was rarely with the main group that included Walker. Green and his party were imprisoned at Perote Castle and the others at Tacubaya. The members of Green's party, especially Henrie, appear prominently in the later portion of his book.

Thomas A. Murry, a native of Ireland and resident of Victoria, was released through the influence of the British minister in Mexico (Green, *Journal*, pp. 201, 441, 445).

William M. Shepherd, born in Virginia and a resident of Liberty, was given special attention by the Mexicans for an act of mercy shown during the battle of Mier. Green records several incidents involving Shepherd, but does not note his ultimate fate. (Ibid., pp. 211, 235, 442.)

Samuel C. Lyon, English born and a resident of Brazoria, was an old friend of Green. Lyon was released from prison September 6, 1844. (Ibid., pp. 127, 219, 440, 477.)

Daniel Drake Henrie was born in Ohio and had been a midshipman in the United States Navy before settling in Brazoria. He escaped from Perote with Green on July 2, 1843. (Ibid., pp. 248, 278–282, 312–366, 439, 446.)

71. As Walker later notes, Dr. Richard Fox Brenham was killed at Salado when the captives made their escape. Brenham was born in Kentucky about 1810 and came to Texas in the summer of 1836. He practiced medicine until 1841, when he joined the ill-fated Texan Santa Fe Expedition. Taken prisoner, he was released and returned to Texas in time to join the Somervell Expedition. The town of Brenham in Washington County is named for him. (*Handbook of Texas*, 1:213.)

72. John Reagan Baker was born in Tennessee on August 6, 1809, and by 1839 was fighting with Ewen Cameron's Rangers in south Texas. In 1841 he was elected sheriff of Refugio County. As Walker later notes, Baker was wounded in the escape at Salado, and was left there. Thus, he did not participate in the drawing of the black beans. Baker was released by the Mexican government on September 16, 1844, and returned to Refugio County, where he went into business. He died near Stockdale, Wilson County, on January 19, 1904, at the age of 94. (*Handbook of Texas*, 1:99–100.)

73. Canfield, in "Mier Expedition" (Day, ed.), p. 174, wrote, "Mr. B was styled a 'Medico' by the Mexicans and I believe was a cook in the federal war in 1839." See also, Day, "Diary," p. 93. Stapp, *Prisoners*, p. 51, called Bullock "a young and very popular American physician" who "came frequently to see us, and displayed his sympathy and solicitude for our comfort, by every kindness and attention compatible with his means and the license allowed him."

74. Walker and most of the other participants were highly critical of Charles K. Reese because he refused to join in the escape attempt. Green, by

contrast, vigorously defended him, possibly because they were prisoners together at Perote and escaped together on July 2, 1843. Certainly Reese's previous record shows him to be brave and honorable. Born in Kentucky on November 13, 1810, he arrived in Texas in time to serve at Gonzales and in the seige of Bexar in the fall of 1835. He fought in the Battle of San Jacinto the following spring. After Reese's escape from Perote, he made his home in Brazoria County, where he died October 14, 1848. (Dixon and Kemp, *Heroes of San Jacinto*, p. 283.) For other critical views of Reese's role in the escape attempt at Salado, see Day, "Mier Expedition," pp. 173, 174, 176; Day, "Diary," pp. 94, 95. For the defense, see Green, *Journal*, pp. 177–178; Wade, *Notes and Fragments*, 2:77–83.

75. George Van Ness, son of Cornelius P. Van Ness, governor of Vermont, came to Texas in 1838 and practiced law in San Antonio with his brother Cornelius. A participant in the Santa Fe Expedition, he was captured and held in Perote Castle until early 1842, but he was back in San Antonio by the time of the Woll raid. He was among those captured by Woll and sent to Mexico. (*Handbook of Texas*, 2:832.) For a firsthand account by a Woll prisoner, see Frederick Chabot, ed., *The Perote Prisoners: Being the Diary of James L. Trueheart.*

76. Philip Dimitt, born in Kentucky about 1801, came to Texas in 1822 and established a frontier trading post, first at San Antonio and then on Lavaca Bay. An early advocate of Texan independence, he helped frame the Goliad Declaration of Independence, December 20, 1835. In the summer of 1841 he and several companions were captured near Corpus Christi Bay by a Mexican raiding party and taken prisoners to Mexico. On September 10 at Hacienda de Agua Nuevo, some of his companions drugged the guard and escaped. The guard threatened to have Dimitt shot unless the other Texans returned, whereupon he killed himself by taking laudanum. (See Joseph Milton Nance, *After San Jacinto: The Texas-Mexican Frontier, 1836–1841*, pp. 445–469.) The definitive account of Dimitt's revolutionary activity is Hobart Huson, *Captain Phillip Dimmitt's Commandancy of Goliad, October 15, 1835–January 1, 1836.* His name is variously spelled.

77. Archibald Fitzgerald was among the Bexar prisoners captured by Woll. In early 1841 he was a private in Jack Hays' spy company, and later that year he joined the Santa Fe Expedition. Captured and imprisoned, he had only recently returned to San Antonio at the time of the Woll raid. He was among the Bexar prisoners who joined the Mier prisoners on January 6, 1943. (Nance, *After San Jacinto*, p. 411; idem, *Attack and Counterattack*, pp. 334, 463, 600.)

John Stansbury, a native of Kentucky and resident of Fort Bend, survived his wound and was among those released by the Mexican government on September 16, 1844 (Green, *Journal*, pp. 442, 477).

78. This portion of the journal was obviously written after Walker conferred with Green, leading to the speculation that the existing manuscript, in part at least, is a copy of the original.

79. Patrick Lyons is listed by Green, *Journal*, p. 440, as a native of Ireland and resident of Milam.

Lorenzo Rice, a native of Maryland, was a resident of San Antonio (Ibid., p. 441).

Green identifies the man whom Walker calls Haggerty as John Higgerson, a native of Ireland who was among the survivors of the Dawson massacre taken prisoner by Woll (Ibid., p. 444). Duval, *Big-Foot Wallace*, p. 203, and Stapp, *Prisoners*, p. 59, agree with Walker that the name was Haggerty but give no further identification.

George Washington Trahern lived to record his own recollections of the expedition. A native of Mississippi, Trahern came to Texas in 1839 and settled at Port Lavaca. He was still only a boy when he enlisted in the Mier Expedition. He was among those prisoners released by the Mexican government September 16, 1844. A brother-in-law of Texas historian Homer S. Thrall, Trahern fought with Sam Walker in the Mexican War and then moved to California, where he amassed a fortune. (See A. Russell Buchanan, ed., "George Washington Trahern: Texas Cowboy Soldier from Mier to Buena Vista," *Southwestern Historical Quarterly* 58 [July 1954], 60–90.)

Thomas Hancock was one of the Bexar prisoners captured by Woll and taken to Mexico. He survived and was released through the influence of Waddy Thompson. (Green, *Journal*, pp. 447, 448; Nance, *Attack and Counterattack*, p. 601.)

John Harvey, a native of Kentucky and resident of Brazoria, also survived. He was released by the Mexican government September 16, 1844. (Green, *Journal*, pp. 439, 476.)

Other firsthand accounts of the escape include Day, "Mier Expedition," p. 176; Day, "Diary," pp. 95–96; Bell, *Narrative*, pp. 26–28; Stapp, *Prisoners*, pp. 57–59.

80. Walker later records the death of John Shipman, a native of Missouri who resided in Fort Bend (Green, *Journal*, pp. 442, 445).

81. Charles K. Reese did indeed act to the best interest of his brother, who was only sixteen years old. Young Billy was released by Santa Anna. (Ibid., p. 193; Wade, *Notes and Fragments*, 2:83.)

82. This portion of Walker's diary is paraphrased in Green, *Journal*, pp. 158 ff.

83. Thomas W. Cox was one of the few men who made good the escape. Born in Alabama in 1785, he emigrated to Texas in 1822. Z. N. Morrell described Cox as "a man of eloquence and great natural ability" who had a "commanding manner and pleasant address," while Houston Wade called him "one of the most peculiar characters that ever lived in Fayette County." A Baptist preacher, Cox was as at home on the battlefield as in the pulpit. He participated in the siege of Bexar in late 1835 and fought at the Battle of San Jacinto and the Plum Creek Fight. He organized several churches in Texas but later became a controversial figure in Baptist circles. (Morrill, *Flowers and Fruits*, pp. 131, 132–133, 144–148; Dixon and Kemp, *Heroes of San Jacinto*, p. 396; Wade, *Notes and Fragments*, 2:84–86.)

84. The brothers Carter and William Sargeant, natives of Kentucky and residents of Bastrop, were generally censured by their comrades. In Day, "Mier Expedition," p. 177, Canfield wrote that "two of our men (who took no part in the charge upon the guard) after securing two of the best horses and provisions deserted their names were Wm. & Carter Sargeant." In Day, "Diary," p. 97, Glasscock made a similar observation and, after the recapture of the entire body of escapees, wrote that "when they left us they went to a rancho, and professed great friendship for the Mexicans stating that they had been forced to fight by our officers at Salado" (p. 100). Walker later notes the reappearance of the brothers and still later records the death of Carter Sargeant in prison. William Sargeant was among those released by the Mexican government September 16, 1844. (Green, *Journal*, p. 447.)

85. Green (*Journal*, p. 442) identifies this man as John Sweizey, originally from Pennsylvania. The name is spelled variously in other accounts, Glasscock giving it as Sweeny (Day, "Diary," p. 97), and Canfield as Sweezy. (Day, "Mier Expedition," p. 177). Walker later notes that the man rejoined the group after all were recaptured.

86. Green identifies the "friend" as a native of New York, while Big-Foot Wallace recalled that the man was an Englishman and an old acquaintance of Cameron. According to George Washington Trahern, the English consul sent the man from Saltillo to give the Texans directions, and J. G. W. Pierson and Cameron had a dispute over whether to trust him. Pierson thought the man had been sent to entrap them, while Cameron did not. Unfortunately, Pierson's view prevailed. (Buchanan, "Texas Cowboy," pp. 63–64; Duval, *Big-Foot Wallace*, p. 206.)

John Brennan was a native of New York who resided at Victoria. He was released from prison September 16, 1844. (Green, *Journal*, pp. 438, 476.)

87. Samuel W. Jordan, a captain in the Texas army 1836–1838, joined with Reuben Ross to aid the Mexican Federalists in 1839. Fighting with Antonio Canales, they attempted to establish the Republic of the Rio Grande. Jordan was in New Orleans in 1841, enlisting men to aid Mexican rebels in Yucatán. Depressed when the boat sailed for Yucatán without him and his recruits, he killed himself with laudanum on June 22, 1841. (*Handbook of Texas*, 1:929; Nance, *After San Jacinto*, pp. 335–360, 399.)

88. Edward Eugene Este later drew one of the black beans. A brother-in-law of David G. Burnet, Este came to Texas from Ohio in 1834 and spent much time at Burnet's home on Buffalo Bayou. Este served briefly in the Texas army but was relieved of duty to assist Burnet. He was with Burnet when Santa Anna reached Morgan's Point shortly before the Battle of San Jacinto and wrote a vivid account of Burnet's narrow escape from the Mexican army. Este's wife, who never joined him in Texas, died shortly after he did, and the family in Ohio apparently never understood the circumstances of his death. Ashbel Smith wrote that Este was "one of the victims of Mexia," and as late as 1950, the historian of the family was still puzzling over the word "Mexia" and did not realize that Este had drawn a black bean. (Edward Nicholas Clopper, *An American Family*, pp. 256–257, 263, 367, 464.)

John Fitzgerald, a native of Ireland and resident of Fort Bend, escaped from Tacubaya about the same time as Walker (Green, *Journal*, p. 446).

The man Walker calls Isam is variously identified in other accounts as Zed Isam or Islam, or T. Iceland or Iseland. German born, he died in prison. (Ibid., p. 439; Bell, *Narrative*, p. 82; Day, "Diary," p. 116.)

89. Robert Michael Pilley was born in England on March 30, 1820. He came to Galveston in the late 1830's and later settled at Harrisburg. He was released from prison September 16, 1844, but never fully recovered from the trials of the Mier Expedition. He married Alice L. Bradbury. Pilley died January 4, 1865, at Bellville. (Wade, *Notes and Fragments*, 1:137.)

90. Mark Rogers, a native of Tennessee and resident of Bastrop, was released from prison September 16, 1844 (Green, *Journal*, pp. 442, 447).

Levi Williams, originally from Missouri, was a resident of Bastrop and also was released September 16, 1844 (ibid., pp. 443, 477).

91. John McMullen, a native of Maryland, was an old acquaintance of Walker and also won renown as a Texas Ranger. He was released from prison September 16, 1844. As a Ranger lieutenant in the Mexican War, he related his experiences in the Mier Expedition to Samuel C. Reid, who recorded them in *Scouting Expeditions*, pp. 30–31, 54–58.

92. Dr. William F. McMath was a native of Georgia and resident of Washington on the Brazos (Green, *Journal*, p. 441; Day, "Mier Expedition," p. 186).

John Tanney, a native of Maryland and resident of Bastrop, was among those released from prison September 16, 1844. He attempted unsuccessfully to escape from Perote March 25, 1844. (John Holmes Jenkins, III, ed., *Recollections of Early Texas: Memoirs of John Holland Jenkins*, pp. 112, 116, 268; Wade, *Notes and Fragments*, 1:133, 2:23, 31–32.)

93. Robert G. Waters, a native of South Carolina and resident of Fort Bend, was released through the influence of Waddy Thompson (Green, *Journal*, pp. 443, 445; Clarence R. Wharton, *History of Fort Bend County*, p. 114).

As Walker later records, James N. Torrey was among those who drew a black bean at Salado. A native of Connecticut, he resided in Harris County, Texas. (Green, *Journal*, pp. 442, 444.)

94. Peter A. Ackerman, a native of New York and resident of Bastrop, almost made good the escape. He was later released from prison on September 16, 1844. (Green, *Journal*, pp. 437, 476; Bell, *Narrative*, p. 80; Wade, *Notes and Fragments*, 1:50.)

95. W. Barney C. Bryan was from Fort Bend (Green, *Journal*, p. 438; Bell, *Narrative*, p. 82).

96. For other accounts of the men's conversion to Roman Catholicism and reactions to it, see Day, "Diary," p. 181; Stapp, *Prisoners*, p. 70.

97. Joseph D. Watkins was a native of Louisiana who resided at Washington on the Brazos. He was released September 16, 1844. (Green, *Journal*, pp. 443, 477.)

E. D. Wright, a native of North Carolina, listed Washington on the Brazos as his Texas residence. He attempted to escape March 24, 1844, but was re-captured and eventually was released September 16, 1844. (Ibid., pp. 443, 450.)

A. J. Lewis was a native of Alabama and resident of Brazoria (ibid., p. 440).

98. The Mexican investigation of the escape placed blame on green troops (Manuel Montero, Matamoras, to Commandant General, February 22, 1843; and Deposition of Lieutenant Colonel Antonio Tenorio, Matamoras, in "Calendar of Documents regarding Mier in National Archives of Mexico," Houston Wade Papers, Archives Division, Texas State Library, Austin).

99. During the Mexican War, the remains of these men were collected by Walter P. Lane and returned to Texas to be buried at Monument Hill, La Grange, alongside those of the victims of the Dawson Massacre (Lane, *Adventures and Recollections*, pp. 67–69).

100. Waddy Thompson agreed with Walker's statement, writing in his memoirs that he regarded the decimation as a much greater atrocity than either the slaughter of the Alamo or the shooting of Fannin's command. "Those prisoners were not on parole, and had a perfect right to escape if they could." (Thompson, *Recollections of Mexico*, p. 73.)

101. John P. Wyatt, a native of Georgia and resident of Fayette County, died in prison on October 30, 1843 (Green, *Journal*, pp. 443, 445; Day, "Diary," pp. 103, 113, 192; Day, "Mier Expedition," p. 181).

Richard Brown, a native of South Carolina and resident of Liberty, was released September 16, 1844 (Green, *Journal*, pp. 438, 476).

102. Samuel McClelland, a native of Ireland, came to Texas in 1835 and fought in Jesse Billingsley's company at the Battle of San Jacinto. He listed his residence as Liberty when he joined the Somervell Expedition. (Green, *Journal*, p. 441; Dixon and Kemp, *Heroes of San Jacinto*, p. 174; Day, "Mier Expedition," p. 182; Day, "Diary," p. 102.)

103. There were four Wilsons on the Mier Expedition. This man was not James Charles Wilson, who, as Walker later notes, joined Walker's party at Santiago on March 26, 1843. James Charles Wilson traveled with another group of prisoners and passed through Tampico.

104. Norman B. Woods was wounded in the Dawson Massacre and taken as a prisoner to Mexico. The son of Minerva and Zadock Woods, he was born in Missouri but came to Texas with his parents in the 1820's. The family settled in Fayette County. Woods married Jane Wells, and they became the parents of five children. Before his death in prison on December 16, 1843, Woods wrote a number of letters describing his experiences. His remains were later buried at Monument Hill, La Grange. (E. W. Winkler, ed., "The Bexar and Dawson Prisoners," *Quarterly of the Texas State Historical Association* 13 [April 1910], 292–324; L. U. Spellman, ed., "Letters of the Dawson Men from Perote Prison, Mexico," *Southwestern Historical Quarterly* 8 [April 1935], 246–269; *Handbook of Texas*, 2:932.)

Thomas Colville was a native of Scotland and a resident of Harris County.

Walker later records his death in prison. (Green, *Journal*, pp. 438, 444; Day, "Mier Expedition," p. 182.)

105. E. J. Kaufman was a native of Tennessee and resident of Bastrop (Green, *Journal*, p. 440).

The brothers Robert B. and William H. Beard, Jr., were born in Arkansas, Robert on February 22, 1806, and William on December 28, 1820. They came to Texas with their parents, who settled first in Fort Bend and then at Seguin. Neither of the brothers survived the expedition. William, in a letter dated May 13, 1843, wrote, "Robert died at San Louis. He suffered a great deal." As Walker later notes, William died a few months later. Both brothers were highly esteemed by their comrades. (Wade, *Notes and Fragments*, 2:43–49.)

106. Philip F. Bowman, a native of New York, was released from prison on September 16, 1844. A resident of Bastrop in 1842, Bowman received $605 for his service in the Mier Expedition on June 25, 1850. During the Mexican War he returned to Mexico as a major in the Pennsylvania First Regiment and again fought with Walker. Upon Walker's death, Bowman received his sword, which he later deposited with the Wyoming Historical and Geological Society at Wilkes-Barre, Pennsylvania. (Green, *Journal*, pp. 437, 476; Dana, *Incidents*, p. 43; Public Debt Papers; Houston Wade Papers.)

Thomas Tatum, a native of Tennessee and resident of Matagorda, was released from prison in late summer, 1844 (Green, *Journal*, pp. 442, 477).

John Mills was a native of Tennessee and resident of Victoria. He was released September 16, 1844. (Ibid., pp. 477, 440.)

Charles Hill, a native of England and resident of Bastrop, did not survive the expedition (ibid., pp. 439, 444; Day, "Diary," p. 104).

John B. Blanton was a native of Georgia and resident of Fayette. Walker later records his death in prison. (Green, *Journal*, pp. 437, 444; Day, "Mier Expedition," p. 185.)

David Overton, a native of Mississippi and resident of Brazos, was released from prison September 16, 1844 (Green, *Journal*, pp. 441, 478; Bell, *Narrative*, p. 81).

Peter Rockyfellow, a native of New York and resident of Jackson County, did not survive the expedition (Green, *Journal*, p. 442).

William P. Stapp survived to write and publish his own account of his trials, but he does not mention being left ill on this occasion. In Day, "Diary," p. 104, Glasscock does mention it.

Benjamin Z. Boone, a native of Missouri, was reputedly a kinsman of Daniel Boone and was among those released from prison September 16, 1844 (Bell, *Narrative*, p. 81; Green, *Journal*, pp. 437, 476; Wade, *Notes and Fragments*, 2:18–34).

James McMicken, a native of Virginia and resident of Victoria, did not survive the expedition (Green, *Journal*, p. 441; Bell, *Narrative*, p. 82; Day, "Diary," pp. 103, 115).

William Wynn, a native of Kentucky and resident of Montgomery, attempted to escape March 25, 1843, but was recaptured (Green, *Journal*, pp. 443, 450).

107. Walker was in the heartland of the Mexican Revolution. Father Miguel Hidalgo sounded the Grito de Delores in this area in 1810 and thus launched the movement that eventually resulted in the independence of Mexico from Spain.

108. Alfred S. Thurmond was among those released September 16, 1844. A native of Tennessee and resident of Victoria, he was fluent in Spanish and had the unpleasant task of reading the decimation sentence to the prisoners at Salado. (Ibid., pp. 442, 477; John Henry Brown, *History of Texas from 1685 to 1892*, 2:247.)

For the location of Huehuetoca, see Antonio García y Cubas, *Atlas Geográfico, Estadístico É Histórico de la República Mexicano*, Carta 16.

109. These men, being separated from the main group, did not participate in the misadventures at Salado. Significantly for Walker, they also followed a different route into Mexico, going first to Tampico, where they were entertained by the United States consul, and then to Mineral del Monte, where they met friendly English and French mineralogists. When Walker escaped from prison, he accompanied two of these men, D. H. Gattis and James Charles Wilson, and they retraced the route and were hastened on their way by the friends at Mineral del Monte and the United States consul. Joseph D. McCutchan was with another party of prisoners that followed after the Wilson-Gattis group. His manuscript "Narrative of the Mier Expedition" traces their adventures (Archives, Rosenberg Library, Galveston). McCutchan was apparently the only captive who took the Tampico route to keep a journal. His manuscript thus supplies information not found elsewhere as to why Walker headed to Tampico and how he knew whom to contact when he escaped.

D. H. Gattis, whom Walker consistently identified as McGattis, was a native of Alabama and resident of Travis County (Green, *Journal*, p. 439; James Charles Wilson, in Wade, *Notes and Fragments*, 2:142–144).

James Charles Wilson spoke on the occasion of the reburial of Walker's remains at the Odd Fellows' Cemetery in San Antonio. Born in Yorkshire, England, on August 24, 1816, Wilson attended Oxford University before emigrating to Texas in 1837. After his return from imprisonment in Mexico, he served as district clerk in Brazoria County, as a representative and a senator in the state legislature, and as an itinerant Methodist minister. He died on February 7, 1861, at Gonzales. Wilson County was named in his honor. (Wade, *Notes and Fragments*, 2:140–144; *Handbook of Texas*, 2:921.)

David Allen was born in Virginia and resided in Harris County, Texas. He was released September 16, 1844 (Green, *Journal*, pp. 437, 476.)

Patrick Usher was born in Ireland in 1801 and came to Texas from North Carolina in 1835. He fought in the Battle of San Jacinto and in December 1836 was elected chief justice of Jackson County. He also represented that county in the Congress of the Republic of Texas. After a lingering illness, Usher died in Perote Castle on August 23, 1843. (Dixon and Kemp, *Heroes of San Jacinto*, p. 200; Jennett, *Biographical Directory*, pp. 182–183; Day, "Mier Expedition," p. 188.)

John Day Morgan was born in England in 1819 but came to the United

States as a child. After residing in Pennsylvania and Louisiana, he came to Texas in 1836. A resident of Bastrop, he joined the Santa Fe Expedition and was taken prisoner but was released in time to enlist in the Mier Expedition. He dropped his last name during the latter to avoid retribution for his prior activities. He participated in the Mexican War and was later a Texas Ranger. Morgan died June 30, 1899. (*Handbook of Texas*, 2:234.) For details of his experiences on the Mier Expedition, see Jenkins, *Recollections*, pp. 107, 120–141. Stapp, *Prisoners*, p. 101, reports his attempted escape.

Harvey W. Sellers, Gilbert R. Brush, and John Christopher Columbus Hill were teenage boys. Sellers, a native of Tennessee and resident of Fayette, and Brush, a native of New York and resident of Fort Bend, were released with the main body of men September 16, 1844. (Ibid., pp. 422, 438, 476, 477; Wharton, *History of Fort Bend County*, pp. 115–117.) Hill, the youngest of the group, joined the expedition with his brother Jeffry and father Asa. As Walker later observes, young Hill attracted considerable attention when he was released and adopted by Santa Anna.

110. George Bibb Crittenden, the prodigal son of Senator John J. Crittenden of Kentucky, was born in 1812 and educated at West Point. After service with the United States army in Arkansas Territory, he resigned his commission and came to Texas, where he enlisted in the Somervell and Mier expeditions. He was released through the influence of his father. He reenlisted in the United States army but continued to bring trouble to himself and his father by his intemperance. During the Civil War he became a general in the Confederate Army while his brother became a general in the Union. His service in the Confederacy was also marked by controversy. (Albert D. Kirwan, *John J. Crittenden: The Struggle for the Union*, pp. 30, 110, 122, 159, 241–242, 446–448; William Preston Johnston, *The Life of General Albert Sidney Johnston*, pp. 396–406.)

111. Henry Journeay, of French descent, was a native of New York and listed his Texas residence as Matagorda. A cabinet maker, he passed the time in prison by making a violin, which is preserved in the Texas State Library. After his release from prison on September 16, 1844, Journeay settled in Galveston. He died in 1876. (Wade, *Notes and Fragments*, 2:97–104; Day, "Mier Expedition," p. 104.)

112. Pratt's assistance was also mentioned in Stapp, *Prisoners*, p. 104, but he is identified only as an American friend in Mexico City who had given generous assistance to the captives.

113. Bimoni Middleton was a native of Illinois and resident of Liberty (Wade, *Notes and Fragments*, 1:129; Day, "Mier Expedition," p. 184; Day, "Diary," p. 105.)

114. The Texas navy, under the command of Edwin Ward Moore, engaged in actions off the coast of Yucatán during April and May 1843 (Tom Henderson Wells, *Commodore Moore and the Texas Navy*, pp. 144–154). Moore disobeyed President Sam Houston's instructions and was proclaimed a pirate for the action. This added to the grievances of the Mier prisoners, and Walker and a group of his fellows issued their own proclamation on July 4, 1843,

supporting Moore and denouncing Houston. (Day, "Mier Expedition," pp. 186–187.)

115. Peter, or Pierre, Menard Maxwell was a scion of the Menard family of Illinois and a kinsman of Michel B. Menard, a founder of Galveston. A special friend of Walker, Maxwell was released with the main body of prisoners on September 16, 1844. (Wade, *Notes and Fragments*, 1:129, 2:145–150.)

116. Wilson M. Van Dyke, a native of Georgia and resident of Jackson, was released September 16, 1844 (ibid., 1:134; Green, *Journal,* pp. 443, 477).

117. John Owen was a native of Pennsylvania and resident of Brazoria (Green, *Journal*, p. 441).

118. In early 1843, the Texas government authorized Jacob Snively to lead an expedition to intercept Mexican traders on the Santa Fe Trail passing through territory claimed by Texas. Snively and his followers engaged in adventures along the northern Texas boundary throughout the summer of 1843 and eventually clashed with United States army troops. (Brown, *History*, 2:287–291; H. Bailey Carroll, "Steward A. Miller and the Snively Expedition of 1843," *Southwestern Historical Quarterly* 54 [January 1951], 261–286.)

119. Robert Smith, a native of Tennessee and resident of Fayette County, was a brother-in-law of Captain William M. Eastland, who drew a black bean. In Day, "Mier Expedition," p. 186, Canfield relates an unflattering anecdote about Smith. See also, Green, *Journal*, p. 442, and Day, "Diary," p. 103.

William Morris was a native of Louisiana and resident of Fort Bend (Green, *Journal*, pp. 441, 445).

120. For other accounts of the prisoners' celebration of July 4, see Day, "Mier Expedition, pp. 186–187; Stapp, *Prisoners*, pp. 97–100; Bell, *Narrative*, pp. 50–51.

Fenton M. Gibson survived to write his own account of the Mier Expedition, of which he was quartermaster. A native of Tennessee, he emigrated to Texas before 1837 and practiced law in Brazoria and later at Richmond. He was released from prison September 16, 1844, and returned to Richmond, where he resumed his law practice and edited a newspaper. (Wade, *Notes and Fragments*, 1:125; Wharton, *History of Fort Bend County*, p. 116.)

121. Santa Anna's adoption of John Christopher Columbus Hill created a flurry of interest then and later. Waddy Thompson writes in his *Recollections*, pp. 76–77, that Hill was a "very shrewd and handsome boy" and relates how he not only won his own liberation but also that of his father and brother. See also, Bell, *Narrative*, p. 50; Day, "Mier Expedition," pp. 192, 193; M. L. Crimmins, "John Christopher Columbus Hill, Boy Captive of the Mier Expedition," *Frontier Times* 28 (June 1951), 253–258. A romanticized account of his life is Fanny Chambers Iglehart, *Boy Captive of the Mier Expedition*.

122. William Ryon or Ryan, a captain of the Mier Expedition, was born in Kentucky on July 3, 1808. He borrowed money from J. P. Schatzell in Matamoros that eased the lot of many of the captives. A resident of Fort Bend, he

was released in the late summer of 1844. (Wade, *Notes and Fragments*, 2: 50–56; Wharton, *History of Fort Bend County*, p. 117.)

There were two men by the name of William Moore on the Mier Expedition.

123. James S. White was a native of Pennsylvania. He died in prison. (Green, *Journal*, pp. 443, 445; Day, "Diary," p. 103.)

124. Willis Copeland, a native of Ohio and resident of Nacogdoches, did not make good this escape attempt. He was released September 16, 1844, however, and wrote his own account of his misadventures. The manuscript is in the Archives Division, Texas State Library, Austin. (Green, *Journal*, pp. 438, 476; Stapp, *Prisoners*, p. 101.)

125. Peter Menard Maxwell wrote Walker relating the reaction to the escape. "After your exit from Tucubay I was closely questioned about my red headed companion or the man who was chained to me. I told them that I had seen the ascension of a baloon on that night and that I believed you were in it bound for Texas. My story was believed as they think there is nothing impossible to a Texiano. I don't think that they made much search for you." (Maxwell to Walker, October 18, 1843, Green Papers.)

Stapp, *Prisoners*, p. 101, gives a view of the reaction that differs from Maxwell's, writing that "a terrible commotion ensued when their departure was discovered; platoons of cavalry being dispatched in all directions in quest of them; their names and descriptions of their persons gazetted, and the police of the capital urged to the most thorough examination of the various lurks of its suburbs. No tidings reached us of the fate of any but Copelin, who was retaken near Matamoras, about a month after his elopement, and brought back to Perote."

126. Walker is cautious about identifying the persons who helped his party escape. When he deposited his journal with Green, most of the Mier men were still prisoners, and those who aided him were still in Mexico and could not afford to have their kindness acknowledged. Some of them can be identified by reading Joseph D. McCutchan's manuscript "Narrative," which follows the course of Gattis and Wilson to Tampico, Mineral del Monte, and thence to Tacubaya. Obviously, they were the ones who knew the route and contacts, and Walker followed their lead. Wilson was cared for by an Englishman for several weeks while he regained his strength. Then he left Mexico on the same vessel that earlier had taken Walker. His account, which first appeared in the Clarksville *Northern Standard*, November 18, 1843, confirms Walker's account but also refrains from identifying those who aided in the escape.

127. Joseph D. McCutchan, in his "Narrative of the Mier Expedition," relates the kindness of Franklin E. Chase, the United States consul in Tampico, to the prisoners. Chase is easily identified by Walker's reference here. Another who especially befriended the prisoners on the Tampico route was a man named Linch, an Irishman. Possibly, he also assisted Walker, Gattis, and Wilson.

128. John Dalrymple was among the Bexar men taken prisoner by Woll. He escaped from Perote with Green on July 2, 1843, but the party separated

to avoid detection. Green and several of the others made their way to Vera Cruz, where friends hastened them on their way. Dalrymple went to Tampico, where he chanced upon Walker. (Green, *Journal*, pp. 312–329, 447; Nance, *Attack and Counterattack*, p. 601.)

129. Walker arrived at New Orleans September 11, 1843, and received considerable attention in the press. "Walker, Wilson, and Gattis were recaptured four times on the road to Tampico," reported the Houston *Morning Star*, September 23, 1843, quoting a New Orleans paper. "The first time they effected their release with a bribe of only one dollar, and the other times by the most trifling stratagems."

BIBLIOGRAPHY

Unpublished Material

Army Papers, Republic of Texas. Archives Division, Texas State Library, Austin.

Thomas Jefferson Green Papers. Southern Historical Collection, University of North Carolina at Chapel Hill.

Kuykendall, J. H. "Sketches of Early Texians." University Archives, Barker Texas History Center, University of Texas at Austin.

McCutchan, Joseph D. "Narrative of the Mier Expedition." Archives, Rosenberg Library, Galveston, Texas.

Public Debt Papers. Archives Division, Texas State Library, Austin.

"Sketch of Colonel John C. Hays, Texas Ranger." From materials furnished by Colonel Hays and Major John Caperton. University Archives, Barker Texas History Center, University of Texas at Austin.

Houston Wade Papers. Archives Division, Texas State Library, Austin.

Books and Articles

Barker, Eugene C., and Amelia W. Williams, eds. *The Writings of Sam Houston.* 8 vols. Austin: University of Texas Press, 1938–1943.

Bell, Thomas W. *A Narrative of the Capture and Subsequent Sufferings of the Mier Prisoners in Mexico.* James M. Day, ed. Reprint. Waco, Tex.: Texian Press, 1964.

Brackett, Albert G. *General Lane's Brigade in Central Mexico.* Cincinnati: H. W. Derby & Co., 1854.

Brown, John Henry. *History of Texas from 1685 to 1892.* Reprint. 2 vols. Austin, Tex.: Jenkins Publishing Co., 1970.

———. *Indian Wars and Pioneers of Texas.* Austin, Tex.: L. E. Daniell, n.d.

Buchanan, A. Russell, ed. "George Washington Trahern: Texas Cowboy Soldier from Mier to Buena Vista." *Southwestern Historical Quarterly* 58 (July 1954), 60–90.

Carroll, H. Bailey. "Steward A. Miller and the Snively Expedition of 1843." *Southwestern Historical Quarterly* 54 (January 1951), 261–286.

Chabot, Frederick, ed. *The Perote Prisoners: Being the Diary of James L. Trueheart.* San Antonio, Tex.: Naylor Co., 1934.

Clarksville *Northern Standard.*

Clopper, Edward Nicholas. *An American Family*. Huntington, W.Va.: Standard Printing & Publishing Co., 1950.

Crimmins, M. L. "John Christopher Columbus Hill, Boy Captive of the Mier Expedition." *Frontier Times* 28 (June 1951), 253–258.

Dana, Edmund L. *Incidents in the Life of Capt. Samuel H. Walker, Texan Ranger*. Wilkes-Barre, Pa.: Proceedings, Wyoming Historical and Geological Society, 1882.

Day, James M. *Black Beans & Goose Quills*. Waco, Tex.: Texian Press, 1970.

———, ed. "Diary of James A. Glasscock, Mier Man." *Texana* 1 (Spring–Summer 1963), 85–119, 225–238.

———, ed. "Israel Canfield on the Mier Expedition." *Texas Military History* 3 (Fall 1963), 165–199.

——— et al. *Rangers of Texas*. Waco, Tex.: Texian Press, 1969.

Dixon, Sam Houston, and Louis Wiltz Kemp. *The Heroes of San Jacinto*. Houston, Tex.: Anson Jones Press, 1932.

Duval, John C. *The Adventures of Big-Foot Wallace*. Macon, Ga.: J. W. Burke & Co., 1870.

García y Cubas, Antonio. *Atlas Geográfico, Estadístico É Histórico de la República Mexicana*. Mexico: José Mariano Fernández de Lara, 1858.

Graham's American Monthly Magazine.

Green, Thomas J. *Journal of the Texian Expedition against Mier*. New York: Harper & Bros., 1845. Reprint, Austin, Tex.: Steck Co., 1935.

———. *Reply of . . . to the Speech of Gen. Sam Houston in the Senate of the United States, August 4, 1854*. Washington, D.C.: n.p., 1855.

Greer, James K. *Colonel Jack Hays: Texas Frontier Leader and California Builder*. New York: E. P. Dutton & Co., 1952.

Gregg, Josiah. *Diary and Letters of . . . : Southwestern Enterprises, 1840–1847*. M. G. Fulton, ed. 2 vols. Norman: University of Oklahoma Press, 1941–1944.

Gunn, Jack W. "Ben McCulloch, Big Captain." *Southwestern Historical Quarterly* 58 (July 1954), 1–21.

The Handbook of Texas. Webb, Walter Prescott, et al., eds. 3 volumes. Austin: Texas State Historical Association, 1952, 1976.

Haven, Charles T. *The History of the Colt Revolver*. New York: Bonanza, 1940.

Hendricks, Sterling Brown. "The Somervell Expedition to the Rio Grande, 1842." *Southwestern Historical Quarterly* 23 (October 1919), 112–140.

House Executive Documents 4, 29 Cong., 2 Sess., Serial 497.

House Executive Documents 60, 30 Cong., 1 Sess., Serial 520.

Houston, Sam. *Speech . . . on Texan Affairs . . . Thomas Jefferson Green*. Washington, D.C.: Congressional Globe Office, 1854.

Houston *Morning Star*.

Houston *Telegraph and Texas Register*.

Huson, Hobart. *Captain Phillip Dimmitt's Commandancy of Goliad, October 15, 1835–January 1, 1836*. Austin, Tex.: Von Boeckmann-Jones Co., 1974.

Iglehart, Fanny Chambers. *Boy Captive of the Mier Expedition.* San Antonio, Tex.: Passing Show Publishing Co., 1910.

Jenkins, John Holmes, III, ed. *Recollections of Early Texas: Memoirs of John Holland Jenkins.* Austin: University of Texas Press, 1964.

Jennett, Elizabeth LeNoir. *Biographical Directory of the Texan Conventions and Congresses, 1832–1845.* Austin, Tex.: n.p., 1941.

Johnston, William Preston. *The Life of General Albert Sidney Johnston.* New York: D. Appleton & Co., 1879.

Kirwan, Albert D. *John J. Crittenden: The Struggle for the Union.* Lexington: University of Kentucky Press, 1962.

Lane, Walter P. *Adventures and Recollections of . . .* Marshall, Tex.: News Messenger Publishing Co., 1928.

Lea, Tom. *The King Ranch.* 2 vols. Boston: Little, Brown & Co., 1957.

Linn, John J. *Reminiscences of Fifty Years in Texas.* New York: D. & J. Sadlier & Co., 1883.

McDowell, Catherine W., ed. *Now You Hear My Horn: The Journal of James Wilson Nichols.* Austin: University of Texas Press, 1967.

Maverick, Mary A. *Memoirs.* San Antonio, Tex.: Alamo Printing Co., 1921.

Morrill, Z. N. *Flowers and Fruits in the Wilderness.* St. Louis: Commercial Printing Co., 1872.

Nance, Joseph Milton. *After San Jacinto: The Texas-Mexican Frontier, 1836–1841.* Austin: University of Texas Press, 1963.

———. *Attack and Counterattack: The Texas-Mexican Frontier, 1842.* Austin: University of Texas Press, 1964.

———, trans. and ed. "Brigadier General Woll's Report of His Expedition into Texas in 1842." *Southwestern Historical Quarterly* 58 (April 1955), 523–552.

Nielsen, George R. "Mathew Caldwell." *Southwestern Historical Quarterly* 64 (April 1961), 478–502.

Oswandel, J. Jacob. *Notes of the Mexican War, 1846–47–48.* Philadelphia: n.p., 1885.

Parsons, John E., ed. *Sam Colt's Own Record.* Hartford: Connecticut Historical Society, 1949.

Reid, Samuel C. *The Scouting Expeditions of McCulloch's Texas Rangers.* Philadelphia: G. B. Zieber & Co., 1847.

Sowell, A. J. *The Life of Big-Foot Wallace.* Bandera, Tex.: Frontier Times, 1927.

Spell, Lota M. *Pioneer Printer: Samuel Bangs in Mexico and Texas.* Austin: University of Texas Press, 1963.

Spellman, L. U., ed. "Letters of the Dawson Men from Perote Prison, Mexico." *Southwestern Historical Quarterly* 8 (April 1935), 246–269.

Stapp, William P. *The Prisoners of Perote.* Philadelphia: G. B. Zieber & Co., 1845. Reprint, Austin: University of Texas Press, 1977.

Thompson, Waddy. *Recollections of Mexico.* New York: Wiley & Putnam, 1846.

Wade, Houston. *Notes and Fragments.* 2 vols. La Grange, Tex.: La Grange Journal, 1936.

Walker, Olive Todd. "Major Whitfield Chalk, Hero of the Republic of Texas." *Southwestern Historical Quarterly* 60 (January 1957), 359–368.

Wallis, Jonnie Lockhart, and Laurance L. Hill, comps. *Sixty Years on the Brazos.* Los Angeles, Calif.: privately printed, 1950.

Webb, Walter Prescott. *The Great Plains.* Boston: Ginn & Co., 1931.

———. *The Texas Rangers: A Century of Frontier Defense.* Boston: Houghton Mifflin, 1935.

Wells, Tom Henderson. *Commodore Moore and the Texas Navy.* Austin: University of Texas Press, 1960.

Wharton, Clarence R. *History of Fort Bend County.* San Antonio, Tex.: Naylor Co., 1939.

Wilson, James Charles. *Address on the Occasion of Removing the Remains of Captains Walker and Gillespie on the 21st of April, A. D., 1856.* San Antonio, Tex.: Ledger, 1856.

Wilson, R. L. *The Arms Collection of Samuel Colt.* Bullville, N.Y.: Herb Glass, 1964.

———. *Samuel Colt Presents: A Loan Exhibition of Presentation Percussion Colt Firearms.* Hartford, Conn.: Wadsworth Atheneum, 1961.

Winkler, E. W., ed. "The Bexar and Dawson Prisoners." *Quarterly of the Texas State Historical Association* 13 (April 1910), 292–324.

INDEX